◆ *How to* ◆
# Ice Climb!

## Craig Luebben

FALCON®

HELENA, MONTANA

*How to Ice Climb*
© 1999 Craig Luebben
All rights reserved. Published in 1999.
Printed in the United States of America.

Cover photo: Dave Sheldon by Craig Luebben.
Inside photos by author unless otherwise noted.

Cataloging-in-Publication Data is on record at the Library of Congress.

# C O N T E N T S

Dick Jackson on an
early ascent of The
Fang, Vail, Colorado.

# Acknowledgments

This book is dedicated to all the partners with whom I've shared a rope, and to all the climbers who have lost their lives teaching us about hazards.

Many thanks to the following climbers who contributed to this book: Joe "Jojo" Josephson made many important additions and corrections, and wrote several sidebars based on lessons he learned as a seasoned ice climber in the grandest arena of all—the Canadian Rockies; Topher Donahue wrote the final two chapters of the book, modeled for and photographed many pictures in Canada, and has been a solid, fun, and safe climbing partner on many grand adventures; John "Verm" Sherman added many valuable thoughts—his literary genius and thoroughness contributed significantly to this effort; Kennan Harvey wrote about alpine ice climbing, contributed several photos, and modeled for some of the more amusing pictures in the book; Kim Csizmazia contributed helpful tips on planting crampons and racking ice protection; Silvia De Vito Luebben was a patient model (she hates to be photographed); Craig DeMartino shot several technique photos; Jake Latendresse reviewed the manuscript, drew the illustrations, helped me test pull dozens of ice screws, pound-ins and hooks, and has served me and other climbers countless "cold ones" in the Town Pump; Duncan Ferguson reviewed some early work on the book, and opened my eyes to the concept of ice climbing like you rock climb.

Thanks also to Mike O'Donnell, Jared Ogden, Mike Kleker, Brad Johnson, Audrey Oberlin, Dave Sheldon, Dave Levy, Phillip Benningfield, and Dave Mitchell, who read the manuscript and offered many important suggestions; Dan Gambino, who helped out by modeling and shooting photos in Vail; Steph Davis, who did some modeling in Pakistan; and Jimmy Surrette and Scott Backes, who provided information about some of the ice climbing areas listed in the final chapter.

Chris Harmston of Black Diamond and Steve Nagode of REI provided ice protection testing information.

In addition, I'd like to thank the following companies: Mountain Hardwear, Black Diamond and Petzl provided equipment or clothing for use during the photo shoots; and Bluewater, Climb High, Excalibur, Pika, Trango, Ushba, and Black Diamond contributed gear to be destroyed in the ice protection tests.

*(opposite page)*
*Stevie Haston cranking out the roof to Octopussy's hanging pillar.*

# Introduction

Twenty years ago, I started ice climbing—solo. Not the wisest thing I ever did, but wisdom was pretty much absent during my youth. I had wanted to take the ice classes offered by master ice climber Duncan Furgeson, but instead spent my money on equipment and beer. Twenty feet up the first climb I planted one axe right next to the other in a bulge. The bulge plated, my tools ripped out, and I decked. The cost of the ER visit and crutches would have easily bought tools, crampons, and Duncan's classes.

In the years following that first day on ice, I gradually became more bold, efficient, and schooled at judging ice. But I still viewed ice technique as primitive—"thunk, thunk, kick, kick," as explained by alpinist John Roskelley. Then, in 1995, I had a discussion with Duncan Ferguson about the finer points of ice climbing. The best techniques for ice climbing, he explained, are the same ones we use rock climbing—stemming, back-stepping, resting, heel hooking, pacing, and the like—using natural features of the ice to climb with poise and efficiency. Add to these rock techniques a potent swing and swift kick, and understanding of ice, and you can climb some horrific ice routes, safely, without getting pumped. Duncan's wisdom, shaped by his 20 years at the cutting edge of ice climbing, gave me a new perspective. This perspective—along with specialized knowledge of ice and equipment, and respect for the ice climbing environment and its hazards—is what I hope to pass along to the reader.

In *How to Ice Climb*, we present techniques for climbing snow and alpine ice, but this is not a snow slogging manual. The focus is waterfall ice and mixed climbing, for climbers of all levels.

Ice climbing in the alpine world requires the ropework of a rock jock, the mountain savvy of an alpinist, the snow knowledge of an avalanche forecaster, and the winter survival skills of an Eskimo. We assume the reader to have knowledge of winter mountain travel, winter survival, rock climbing techniques, and climbing ropework. Climbers with beginning or rudimentary rock climbing skills should study *How to Rock Climb* by John Long to get up to speed. Those lacking in-depth information on snow climbing, glacier travel, mountain navigation, avalanche safety, and other alpine skills should consult the references in the bibliography, especially *Mountaineering: Freedom of the Hills*.

To provide a variety of perspectives, *How to Ice Climb* includes contributions by several professional climbers: adventurer and photographer Kennan Harvey wrote the alpine snow and ice chapter; world traveler and alpine guide Topher Donahue wrote the hazards and North American ice chapters; champion athlete and accomplished ice climber Kim Csizmazia wrote about planting your crampons and dealing with the rack; Canadian ice pioneer Joe Josephson wrote numerous sidebars; and master of sarcasm and bouldering guru John Sherman chronicled his lessons from several ice climbing aces. Their contributions make the book more readable, entertaining, and informative.

Throughout this book, we stress a conservative approach to ice climbing. Especially during the apprenticeship, be humble to avoid getting in over your head. But once you gain confidence, technique and experience, once you are a *rad* ice climber, then go for it—uncage yourself and push some limits. The beauty of climbing is in leaving the doldrums of the modern world and in experiencing life far more intensely.

## LEARNING FROM THE PROS

*by* John Sherman

Why did Craig Luebben ask me, a climber whose reputation is based on cranking boulder problems and upsetting the prudish, to contribute to a book on ice climbing? It certainly wasn't based on my ice climbing résumé. On the contrary, when it comes to ice climbing I'm probably a lot like you, eager to learn all I can on the subject and improve my skills so that I might climb classics such as *Ames Ice Hose*, *Polar Circus*, or *Slipstream*. Perhaps unlike you, I have had the great fortune to climb with some of the world's top ice climbers, some of whom have contributed to this book—climbers like Mark Wilford, Joe Josephson, Barry Blanchard, Guy Lacelle, Scott Backes, Charlie Fowler, and Bruce Hendricks. And yes, I've even climbed with Craig, who's no slouch himself.

One of my first multi-pitch ice climbs was the Canadian classic *Bourgeau Left Hand*, which a friend and I climbed with famed ice stud Barry Blanchard. The first pitch was mere inches thick and poorly bonded to the rock, something like a necktie draped over a fat man's belly. Watching Barry lead, I learned patience. I don't mean me not fidgeting at the base, I'm talking about Barry taking his time, making sure every placement was solid before moving to the next. He absolutely refused to climb himself into trouble by taking any section of the pitch lightly. Every swing was premeditated, every sketchy placement tested. The rest of the climb remained fantastic—the belay cave you could park a VW in, the final vertical curtain—so much so we lost track of time and ended up racing darkness to get to the base. During the descent I learned more from Barry. He misjudged the length of the penultimate rappel, thinking we could rap two pitches in one with our 200-foot ropes. After setting an intermediate anchor, I rapped past him in the dark. He was suspended from three tools in 2 inches of ice. "It feels a lot thicker when it's dark," he said. I made a mental note to keep track of pitch lengths in the future. Better to learn from his mistakes than my own.

Climbing with Scott Backes drove the point home about staying in control at all times. We were climbing a barely formed *Jaws* in Rocky Mountain National Park. As Scott climbed the

Guy Lacelle on the first ascent of Le Grand Delire, in the Gaspesie region of Quebec.
JOE JOSEPHSON PHOTO

pillar, I was impressed at how well he aimed his tools, how he'd focus on the point he wanted to hit, not the vicinity, and stab the pick exactly there. The pillar looked like the crux, but once atop it, Scott found himself face-to-face with a 1-inch sheet of low angle ice. Between that ice and the rock beneath was an eighth-inch of swirling and bubbling water. The stretch was only a few moves long: In 15 seconds he could scamper up it and get to thicker ice above. The temptation must have been great to risk these few moves and get it over with quick. Scott resisted the sirens, and spent the better part of an hour arranging protection in the nearby rocks. I learned that if there was any doubt as to the integrity of the ice, you must do everything you can to protect yourself. Even when the ice was thick elsewhere, I noticed that Scott would hack away until he reached good ice. "Go ahead and cut for 15 minutes if that's what it takes," he told me. This advice came in handy a year later in Canada. I found myself 70 feet up a sun-rotted waterfall. The surface ice was like styrofoam: easy to climb, but too soft to hold a screw. I carved over a foot deep looking for good ice that would take a screw, but found only brittle chandeliered icicles. I spent well over 15 minutes excavating with no luck. Perhaps the ice above would have remained easy, but without pro, the risk seemed excessive so I downclimbed.

Amongst other things, Mark Wilford taught me to keep my heels low, and not to over-swing lest I waste energy both placing and removing tools. I also learned that when your partner is driving 90 miles per hour on snow-packed roads, the best way to get him to accelerate is to ask him to slow down. Duncan Ferguson clued me into sideways placements in thin ice and using all the flex my boots allow. He also provided a model of elegance and efficiency to aspire toward. Joe Josephson has the coolest head I've seen, Charlie Fowler the most impressive ax swing, and Guy Lacelle the healthiest attitude. And last, but not least, watching Duane Raleigh stumble through the forest convinced me to always keep a headlamp in my pack.

One thing I've noticed is that all the top ice climbers do things differently. What makes them so good is that they found a system that worked for them, and stuck with it. Throughout this book you may read conflicting advice. There is no single best way to climb ice. Instead, the best way to climb ice is the way that works best for you. When I first saw *Polar Circus*, I nearly wet my pants. By adopting and adapting the advice of my mentors, I found myself standing atop it a year later, having lead every pitch.

I've been lucky to have such mentors. With this book, you too will benefit from their experiences, and those of other top climbers. And though they all have their own unique way of climbing ice, there is one bit of advice that every pro I've climbed with has told me. When they hear my pick clumsily bounce off the rock beneath a thin sheet of ice, they all say, "Just swing harder. It'll stick."

# The Ice Climbing Game

# CHAPTER 1

*"If you think ice climbing is crazy, then you shouldn't do it."*

Ice forms two ways in the mountains: *alpine ice* falls as snow and, over time, consolidates into hard-packed snow, neve, or blue ice; while *water ice* forms where runoff, meltwater, and seepages freeze into temporary suspension.

Water ice is a deliciously varied medium—it forms sheets, smears, pillars, bulges, grooves, icicles, roofs, cones, chandeliers, and cauliflowers, and ranges from the hardness of concrete to the consistency of ice cream. Throw in some rock and you've got a wild range of climbing possibilities—a frozen world of fun, fear, and adventure.

With adventure comes danger. Just ask all my friends who have died in the mountains. Many hazards imperil the ice climber—sharp tools, frigid temperatures, blinding storms, avalanches, falling ice, unstable formations, bad protection and long runouts. At least the beer doesn't get warm. If you prefer a safe, heated, rock gym to shear terror and frozen fingers—good call. Otherwise, read on and proceed with caution.

## THE ICE EVOLUTION

As a sport, ice climbing is continually evolving. Its known roots date back more than two centuries, to shepherds tending their flocks in the Alps. The earliest alpine ice climbs arose out of necessity—the shepherds needed mobility in the mountains to tend their flocks. They designed rudimentary crampons and ice axes for early-season snow and ice slopes. As far as we know, ice climbing for sport began when rich Englishmen hired the shepherds to guide them to the summits of the Alps. As early as 1786, such a team reached the 15,781-foot, snowy summit of Mont Blanc. Over the next two centuries, standards rose steadily, driven by equipment innovations and increasing confidence, to the point where today, almost any ice face or smear is climbable.

The challenges offered by steep, frozen waterfalls weren't tapped until the 1970s. During the late 1970s and early 1980s waterfall climbing caught on, and the new equipment became widely available. Dozens of ice climbing pioneers made advancements on many fronts: the Canadian Rockies, Scotland, Colorado, New England, California, Quebec, the French and Italian Alps, and Norway.

With a perfect climate and geography for frozen waterfalls, North America's best concentration of big, classic gems was found in the Canadian Rockies. The Rockies became the ice climber's mecca, with waterfall and alpine ice routes unrivaled in North America.

*Ezio Marlier pulling through a roof of hanging icicles on the first ascent of Culture Shock, Val d'Aosta, Italy.*

As standards, techniques, and equipment advanced, climbers took their skills and confidence to the high mountains, pushing limits on routes from Alaska to Peru, and from the Alps to the Himalayas.

In mountaineering, climbers often confronted both rock and ice climbing at the same time. Hence, mixed climbing was born. In the mid-1990s, with more climbers than ever decked out in ice gear, the spotlight shifted to short, hard mixed routes. With the influx of new climbers, manufacturers have continued innovating and improving ice gear. Today, the sport of ice climbing includes alpine faces, huge and small; waterfalls of all angles, shapes and sizes; thin, desperate, hard-to-protect testpieces; hanging pillars; and gymnastic, bolt-protected rock climbs with a few specks of ice. Now the sport is splintering, with traditional ice and mixed climbing on one hand, and pre-protected, sport ice and mixed routes on the other. This incredible diversity presents many opportunities for climbers.

To explore a more complete history of ice climbing, check out Chouinard's *Climbing Ice*, and Jeff Lowe's *Ice World*.

*"Good judgment comes from experience, and experience comes from bad judgment."*

Experience, control, and good judgment are critical to survival in the cold, cruel world of ice climbing; yet they come only with mileage on ice. A thorough study of this book and the other recommended works can fast-track you through some of the difficulties that beginners struggle with. Don't do it the way I did by teaching myself and screwing up big time. Instead, beginners should start off right by learning from a *qualified* ice climbing guide. Nothing can substitute for the knowledge and experience gained by learning from a seasoned guide—this book only supplements good instruction. In addition, learn from as many good climbers as you can, then take what you like from each one and develop your own style.

Ice climbing enters the competition arena. The speed climbing event at ESPN's winter Extreme Games.

Just because someone calls himself or herself a guide doesn't mean that person is any good. And a good rock guide doesn't necessarily make a good ice guide. Seek someone with credentials, like certification by the American Mountain Guides Association (AMGA), Association of Canadian Mountain Guides (ACMG), International Federation of Mountain Guides' Associations (IFMGA), or employment by a top-notch guide service. Make sure they've paid their dues on ice, and can easily lead high standard ice routes, or you'll likely receive mediocre instruction.

For information on how to contact the AMGA and get a list of certified guides, see the Appendix.

Before stepping out on the sharp end, toprope and follow many climbs, and practice setting ice anchors—leading ice is serious business. Learn the many nuances of ice climbing before putting your life on the line.

## HOW HARD IS IT?

Ice is difficult to grade accurately because it changes over the course of a season, from year to year, and sometimes even from morning to afternoon. Early season ice is often thin, sometimes poorly bonded, and generally follows the contours of the cliff. These can be the most physically and mentally demanding conditions. As the season progresses, cascades usually fill out; often the bottom gets fatter than the top, so the overall steepness decreases. Other routes sublimate away (the ice turns directly to vapor) and vanish into air by mid-season.

Busy routes get peg-boarded with axe holes and footsteps, which can knock a stout testpiece down to a beginner's romp. Some routes are elusive and only form every few years, while others may be fat and easy one year then thin and desperate the next. In the morning a climb might be brittle, strenuous and scary, but by afternoon it's plastic and cruiser. Or it might be plastic in the morning and vertical slush by afternoon—direct sunshine wreaks havoc on ice. The fear factor also throws ratings off—a climb that's simple on toprope may be horrifying on lead, paralyzing the leader's ability to climb efficiently and safely.

All these caveats aside, the North American ice grading system currently rates the technical difficulty of ice from 1 to 8. Mixed routes go to 10, with another number grade being added almost every season. Adding the prefix AI, WI, or M designates alpine ice, water ice, or mixed rock and ice, respectively. WI1 is a rating that rarely gets used, like 5.1 in the rock grading system. WI2 is super-low angle and usually not very interesting to climb. WI3 is a good beginning grade, with angles varying from 50 to 75 degrees. WI4 ranges from 70 to 80 degrees, with maybe a short vertical stretch.

Though a direct comparison is difficult to make, and may mislead some good rock climbers into a false sense of their ability on ice, WI4 might require a skill level comparable to 5.9 rock, for a climber who is adept on ice and rock. WI5 has extended sections of vertical ice so it can be pumpy and technical.

*(opposite page)*
*Nemesis, Alberta, Canada.*

This grade might correspond to 5.10 or easy 5.11 rock, although some strong rock climbers, less experienced on ice, have told me they get more pumped on WI5 than on 5.12. Likewise, some ice climbers who crank out the hardest ice routes in the world can barely climb rock harder than 5.10. For this reason, I was warned not to compare rock and ice grades, but I couldn't resist. With the burgeoning popularity of ice climbing, many WI5 routes feel more like WI3+ or 4 by mid-season, after they're pock-marked full of pick holes and footholds.

WI6, is overhanging, technical, brutally continuous, and potentially dangerous (in truth, all ice is potentially dangerous). Unlike sport climbing, the risk on ice climbs often increases with difficulty, because the structures become more precarious and difficult to protect. The challenge on such routes lies not only in physical difficulty, but also in fleshing out protection, controlling your fear, and climbing with flawless technique so you don't fall.

On the other hand, the recent introduction of sport ice climbs, pre-protected with bolts and pitons, has created routes where the difficulty is primarily physical.

WI7 and WI8 are the current top standards for pure ice routes. Imagine ice moves comparable to 5.12 rock, with horrendous protection and a suspicion that everything could tumble down at any moment. On *Cohesion Zero*, a WI7 in Val d'Aosta, Italy, the crux fourth pitch was a hanging sheet of icicles so precarious that the leader Ezio Marlier could not get his picks to stick in the ice. Instead, he punched holes in the ice sheet, inserted his ice axes through the holes, and toggled them sideways for the shaft to catch on the icicles. Climbing in this manner without protection for the first 50 feet, Marlier spent three hours piecing together the 120-foot pitch. He says, "it was the worst time of my life." Compare this sustained, life-risking effort to climbing a bolt-protected, one-pitch M7 with a 10-foot crux, and you begin to see the shortcomings of the rating system.

Mixed climbing has traditionally involved moving through short stretches of rock or frozen moss to link up sections of water ice, or combining the techniques of rock and ice climbing to get up a desperately thin piece of ice. Mixed routes are graded by combining a rock grade with an ice grade, or by using the relatively new M grade. Again, it's tough to make perfect grading comparisons, but to me M4 feels like 5.8, M5=5.9, M6=5.10, M7=5.11, and M8=5.12. Jojo says the mixed grades here correspond to off-width rock grades, so watch out. Beyond M9, it's still being sorted out.

In some areas, mixed routes are graded by joining an ice grade with a rock grade. For example, *Bullwinkle* in the Canadian Rockies receives a grade of 5.10 WI4. A more modern system combines the M scale with the WI scale. For example, *Damage Control*, a mixed route in Val d'Aosta, receives a grade of

WI5+ M7, which tells you that the pure ice climbing is graded 5+, and the rock (or mixed) climbing on the route is 7. Some climbers would drop the WI5+ from the grade and just call it M7.

The mixed climbing game has branched into new specialties. Some of the newer routes climb horrendously difficult, over-hanging rock, with short sections of comparatively trivial ice along the way. Most of these routes are pre-protected with bolts, pitons or fixed nuts. This new deviation relates more to sport climbing than ice climbing.

On complex routes you can combine grades to cover all the styles of climbing involved. A fairly long, engaging route in the Canadian Rockies, *The Day After les Vacances de Monsieur Hulot*, is graded 270m, V, 5.9, A2, WI6. The length of the route is given first: 270 meters. The commitment grade, given next, ranges from I to VII. (In this case, V means the route is a fairly serious

*Alberta, Canada's famous trio on Mount Rundle: The Terminator, The Replicant, and Sea of Vapors.*

undertaking, but not extreme.) The ice commitment grade is more complex than the Roman numeral grade given to rock climbs. In the case of rock climbs, the commitment grade mostly measures the time spent on a route, with I representing minimal time and commitment, and VII representing a very committing, multi-day route. For ice climbs, the commitment grade also includes the seriousness, difficulty, sustained nature, objective hazard, and length of the approach and descent of any given route.

For its free climbing and aid climbing on rock, *Monsieur Hulot* also receives a 5.9 A2 grade. Usually the rock grade assumes that you're wearing crampons and gloves. Armed with rock shoes and climbing bare-handed, the same pitch might be 5.7 or so (though I have been assured that on this route the rock climbing would be harder than 5.7, even with rock shoes). Finally, the difficulty of the ice climbing on the route is WI6, meaning it's fairly serious, especially in hard condition. An R or X can be added to a grade to warn of danger on a route. R means the protection is not great; you could get seriously hurt if you fall. X means the leader risks a lethal fall on the route because little or no protection exists, or the whole pillar could come tumbling down—with you on it. In reality, most climbers assume that any ice climb is R- or X-rated, because you never want to fall. Different guidebooks and articles use all or part of this grading system, as appropriate for their area. Often, shorter ice routes receive only a WI or M grade.

Some climbers who have put a lot of their life energy and psyche into ice climbing have become infuriated at others who climb a desperate route when it's in easy condition, then claim the ascent at the stated grade. For example, during the winter of 1996–1997, the Canadian Rockies WI7 testpiece *Sea of Vapors* came in fat and (relatively) easy. It received dozens of ascents that year, and though it was in WI5 condition, many ascensionists claimed WI7, leading some climbers to nickname the route *Sea of Posers*. The new Canadian Rockies guidebook will list such routes with a variable grade, such as *Sea of Vapors* WI5-7. It's best to be honest about your accomplishments and the conditions you found, but in the end, the most important person not to fool about your ability is yourself.

If all this discussion of grades has left you confused, don't worry. Grades are merely a tool to compare the relative difficulty of ice routes. Always use the current conditions and appearance of a route to judge what you're getting into. Also, beware that grades are often specific to the areas in which they are used. WI5 in one area may be far more difficult than WI5 in another, so it's good to spend some time getting to know a new area before pushing your limits. See the 1998 *American Alpine Journal* for an in-depth comparison and discussion of various waterfall ice rating systems. At any rate, avoid getting caught up in the numbers game; rather, choose routes based on their beauty, adventure, and your ability to lead them safely. Climbing is about having fun and challenging yourself, not keeping score like golf, baseball or bowling.

# APPROACHING ICE CLIMBS

How you approach the ice is a personal choice, depending on snow conditions, the steepness and length of the approach, and the availability of skis or snowshoes. In early season, before much snow has accumulated, it's often easiest to walk to the ice. Ditto for short, or really steep, or icy approaches. Once snow has accumulated, skiing is often the fastest, most efficient and fun way to access ice climbs, especially if you have a long approach. Skiing with a pack full of ice gear can be trying, so good skiing skills are important, especially in avalanche terrain. If you lack adequate skiing ability, or have to approach through densely wooded or brushy terrain, snowshoes may be the ticket.

Once a good ski track has been made, it's inconsiderate to post-hole the trail by walking on it. Either come prepared with skis or snowshoes, or walk off to the side, so you don't destroy the ski track. This is especially important on prepared ski tracks, such as in Vail, where access could be denied based on climbers repeatedly trashing the piste.

For ski approaches, skis fitted with randonee bindings that clamp onto your ice boots are the way to go. Medium to long skis work well on long, flat approaches, or in deep powder. Short to medium-length skis work best on switchbacked trails, densely wooded terrain, or for those with moderate skiing ability. Whether you're skiing, snowshoeing, or walking, a good pair of ski poles keeps you balanced, and lets your arms assist in the approach. If you'll be approaching through avalanche terrain, choose adjustable poles that convert into avalanche probes, and don't forget the avalanche beacons.

Snowshoeing is the way to go if the approach is too steep or wooded for skis.

## TAKING RESPONSIBILITY

Self-reliance is the name of the game in the mountains. All climbing teams should be prepared to take care of themselves if things go wrong. Avoid being rescued. It's bad form, and it puts others in jeopardy. Many rescue teams are marginally prepared to conduct a vertical rescue, especially on ice, so you're putting yourself and them at risk by calling for a rescue. In remote mountain locations, or during bad weather, a rescue may not even be possible, or it may arrive too late to keep you alive. Take responsibility—use good judgement and good technique to avoid epics, and deal with problems yourself.

Knowledge of self-rescue techniques and first aid is crucial for responsible climbing. Self-rescue techniques are covered thoroughly in *Advanced Rock Climbing* by John Long and myself, and *Self Rescue* by David Fasulo (both books are available from Falcon Publishing). To have a prayer of using self-rescue techniques effectively, you must practice them beforehand. A Wilderness First Responder course and CPR certification is the minimum medical training that serious climbers should have. Is your medical training up to snuff? Do you understand the principles of self-rescue (especially escaping the belay, and ascending the rope to free it if it snags during a rappel)? If not, spend your time boning up on these critical skills before heading out to climb in the cold, cruel world of ice. And don't forget the first-aid kit.

Even more important than knowing how to deal with bad situations is avoiding them in the first place. Climb conservatively, lead like you're soloing, and spend whatever effort it takes to place good protection. Often, getting good protection on a lead is the crux of the climb. Read this book thoroughly, and heed the safety tips laced throughout. **It's really easy to die or get maimed ice climbing if you're not constantly evaluating conditions and thinking about safety.**

If you travel in glaciated areas, it's also essential to know crevasse rescue techniques, and to be prepared to pull them off. *Glacier Travel and Crevasse Rescue* by Andy Selters is required reading here, and for inexperienced climbers, a glacier travel course from a reputable guide service is highly recommended. Crevasses are like hidden land mines—stay roped up and know the tricks and you can overcome most of the hazard.

Likewise, it's totally irresponsible to be an ice climber and not have an understanding of avalanche safety. More ice climbers (and backcountry skiers) die in avalanches than by any other mountain hazard. We briefly cover avalanche safety in chapter 9, but we cannot devote the whole book to avalanche safety. If you desire to make informed decisions in the winter wonderlands rather than rolling the dice every time you go out, take an extensive avalanche course, *and* study the avalanche texts listed in the bibliography. Shoulder the greatest respect for this demon which has taken so many of our comrades, or you might join them.

A special note to beginners: it's crucial for each climber on the team to share responsibility for keeping the team safe and self-reliant. This means being knowledgeable about climbing anchors and ropework. If you're always relying on your partners to set things up for you, what are you going to do if they get hurt? Seek professional instruction if you're a beginner, or if you have glaring weaknesses, such as poor climbing technique or rope skills. A few classes will make you safer, more knowledgeable, and improve your technique on the ice, and all of this will make ice climbing much more fun. Most importantly, use good judgement and climb *carefully*.

## SPEED IS SAFETY

Starting out on those first few one- or two-pitch ice climbs, you should take all the time you need to place lots of ice screws and to get up and down safely. As your skills improve and the routes get longer, however, the old alpine climber's adage *speed is safety* starts to become relevant. The idea is to move light and fast in the mountains, to lessen your exposure to objective hazards such as storms, avalanches, and falling rocks and ice, and to ensure that you're up and off the route before nightfall. If you carry a huge amount of gear, you'll move slow, and increase your exposure to these objective hazards. If you always place protection every 10 feet, you'll certainly be benighted if you try a 300-meter long route.

If you hope to become an alpine ace, pare your pack to the essential gear, learn how to climb solidly without overprotecting, and get fit so you can move out. Start your climbs early to utilize the winter's meager daylight hours, and move steadily at a pace you can maintain all day long. Choose partners that you can trust through thick and thin (ice, that is).

## THE CROWDED CLIFFS WE CLIMB

Many popular ice climbing areas have become overcrowded in the past few years, a condition that's often frustrating, inconvenient, and dangerous. Last year at an ice festival I saw people dropping ice all over each other, climbers soloing above others, people sketching on lead who had no business on the sharp end, other climbers trusting really poor anchor setups, and one belayer who fell 10 feet, along with his climber, because he wasn't tied tight to his anchors. In Boulder Canyon, Colorado, two ice climbers battled over a route with ice axes, making all climbers look like a tribe of deranged morons.

Clearly we don't have enough ice to accommodate the masses who want to climb it. Creation of more ice parks may relieve the crowding, or it may worsen the situation by drawing more people into the sport. What's a climber to do?

My personal solution has been to climb less in the local, crowded Colorado areas, and instead travel to less populated areas where I focus my ice season into a few concentrated weeks. Obviously, not everyone has this luxury, but you can often avoid the crowds by getting up wicked early, climbing on weekdays, making long approaches to less popular ice routes, or

*The author on the cauliflower ice start of Rigid Designator, Colorado (WI3 + -5)*

CRAIG DeMARTINO PHOTO

seeking out the obscure. Most importantly, we have to exhibit patience and courtesy with our fellow climbers, and we have to share the ice. Climbing is about having fun, challenging ourselves, and experiencing camaraderie with our fellow climbers. It's not about expressing animosity and making nasty comments when others share our goals.

# *Equipment*

# CHAPTER 2

*"Gear does not a climber make."*

Getting decked out for ice climbing is an expensive proposition. Boots, crampons, and ice tools alone can set you back a cool grand. Head-to-toe pile insulation, a waterproof and breathable shell, a rack of ice screws, rock pitons and ice hooks, and approach skis can run even more. Avoid the temptation to be cheap when assembling your arsenal, though—your life rides on your gear and clothing.

For the most part, the available gear performs its job. Skill and experience is far more important than your brand of equipment. Admittedly, evolutions in ice gear have made the sport easier and safer, helped standards advance, and made the sport more accessible to beginners.

In this chapter we only describe the equipment needed for ice and mixed climbing. How to use it comes later.

## HELMET

A good helmet is standard ice climbing gear. Wear one and smile every time a small piece of ice pops you in the head. Put your helmet on *before* you reach the base of the ice flow or any other vertical terrain. John Sherman was nearly killed by falling ice within the 60 seconds that it took him to don his helmet at the base of a route near Banff, Canada.

The stooge. This climber WILL take a blow to the head unless he wisens up and starts wearing a helmet.

Falling ice is a given, and it often seems to land on your head. Any ice climber who likes his or her brain should wear a helmet, no matter how many photos you've seen of ice heroes climbing foolishly sans helmet.

Some helmets even come with a retractable visor, to protect your eyes from flying ice and your face from the adze of a poorly set axe.

## ICE TOOLS

"You'll regret it," my partner Topher predicted as I chose unfamiliar tools for our ascent of *Virtual Reality,* a WI6 route laced with giant dripping icicles in the Canadian Rockies. "I can swing any of these tools just fine," I cockily replied.

I should have known better. On ice, your ice tools become extensions of your body. As you climb with a certain tool you learn its intricacies and fine-tune your technique. Put a strange tool in your hands and it will often feel awkward and clumsy.

Soloing the approach pitch on *Virtual Reality,* the picks repeatedly got stuck, and I battled to remove them. Following the WI5 third pitch, I abruptly pitched off when both picks ripped. This would never have happened with my tried-and-true axes. Leading *My Daddy's a Psycho* later that day, the initial thin curtain of ice provided sketchy protection. I overprotected, overgripped, overplanted, and constantly stuck the axes, and ultimately got pumped out of my gourd. I was baffled that other climbers said they liked these tools. The moral: the best tools are probably the ones you're used to.

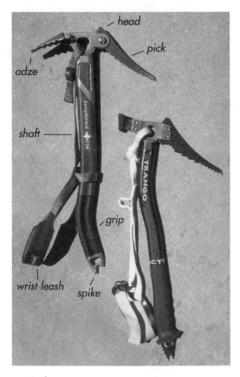

Ice Tool

The crop of modern ice tools.

Ice tool manufacturers have made vast improvements in their designs over the past decade. The best modern tools are easier to place and remove, more secure, and create less vibration than their predecessors, permitting skilled climbers to make climbing more artful and less brutish, and allowing beginners to hack their way up former testpieces. Arming yourself with the best tools gives you an edge, but to safely lead hard ice you still need technique, fitness, experience, and mental control. Anyone who says ice climbing is easy hasn't climbed hard routes in hard conditions.

An ice axe is the ultimate multipurpose tool. You can plant it in the ice, grab rock edges, divots, or cracks, hack away ice to create a ledge, drive in pitons or pound-ins, chop a starting hole for an ice screw, use it like a cane for balance, sink the shaft into hard snow for an anchor, and self arrest if you slip on a snowfield.

With all these uses, and the amazing variety of designs, each tool has its strengths and weaknesses. When choosing a tool, consider the types of climbing you'll be doing, your body size, and style. Tools should be sized somewhat proportionately to your body size. The smaller you are, the lighter, shorter, and thinner-gripped your tools should be. The more aggressively you swing your tools, the heavier they should be.

For alpine climbing, simplicity rules. Go for straight or mildly bent shafts with leashes that attach at the head of the axe, and avoid molded grips or funky spikes. You'll probably want one tool with a hammerhead, and the other with an adze. A stout head is good for pounding the shaft into hard snow for an anchor, and driving pins and pound-ins.

If you climb waterfalls in an alpine environment, you'll frequently appreciate the attributes of a good alpine tool; in a cragging environment, all the fancy gizmos like radically bent shafts, molded hand grips, detachable leashes, and leashes attached midshaft start to make

As a cane on low angle ice or snow.

Planting the shaft into snow.

The dagger, for rapid climbing on hard snow.

*Setting the picks in water ice.*

*Dry tooling for purchase on rock.*

*Chopping a ledge with the adze.*

*An adze placement in rotten ice.*

*The adze cammed for purchase in a crack.*

sense. For mixed climbing, most waterfall tools work fine, provided the pick is properly "ramped" (see Tuning your Pick below). Here, adzes and hammerheads that cam and jam in cracks show their utility, and special dry-tooling claws might be useful.

Most waterfall tools and many alpine axes are modular, so you can change or replace picks, hammerheads, and adzes. You'll be happier replacing a pick than buying a new tool when the pick breaks or wears out. General-use snow axes are one piece.

You can garner a lot of information about ice tools from magazine reviews, but what works best for you is definitely a personal choice, so it's good to test tools before you buy. The trouble is, most tool demos and ice festivals feature hacked-up, too-warm ice, where any tool works well. The trick is to sick the tools on cold, brittle, virgin ice, to see how well they really work.

Try borrowing a friend's, or demo them from a shop that actually lets you take them out.

## Picks

Picks are your front-line connection to the ice. A good pick penetrates ice like cheesecake, holds securely, cleans with ease, and is durable, even at arctic temperatures. An effective pick makes a mediocre tool workable, while a bad pick makes a great tool terrible. For some unexplainable reason, most out-of-the-box picks must be modified to give acceptable performance.

*A blade pick buried securely in the ice.*

Fortunately, tuning your picks doesn't take long. The biggest problem with most stock picks is the blunt front profile. These work fine in plastic, hacked-up ice, but in brittle conditions you'll chop half the climb away before getting the pick to stick. A nice, pointy pick enters the ice clean. For easy removal, bevel the teeth and the top of the pick. Finally, a ramp behind the front point adds security when dry tooling.

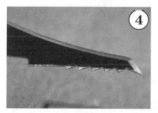

*1. A factory pick.*
*2. Sharpen the front edge of the pick.*
*3. File a ramp behind the front point if you'll be dry tooling.*
*4. Bevel the teeth and top edge of the pick.*

### Tuning Your Pick

Ice climbers should tune their picks with the same care that downhill ski racers tune their skis. Even most factory-new picks need a tune-up before climbing. Tune and sharpen your picks with a medium or fine hand file; using a power grinder risks overheating the metal and destroying the temper of the metal, leaving the pick with the stiffness of a coat hanger.

To tune your pick:

• Put a sharp, pointy edge on the front edge of the pick for good ice penetration.

• Even out any low or high spots on the bottom teeth so they grab the ice equally, and make sure all teeth are sharp.

• Ramp the lower edge just behind the pick for dry tooling.

• Bevel the teeth and the top edge of the pick for easier removal. After you file the top edge razor sharp, run the file horizontally across it to dull the edge just a bit, so it doesn't deform when you try to slice it through the ice.

Some of my Canadian friends break several picks each season. They say it's the bitter cold, but I think it's because their forearms are bigger than my calves. When leading, it's good practice—some would say essential—to carry a third tool in case you break a pick or drop a tool. Always check your picks for tightness before launching up a route. If you do forgo the third tool, a spare pick and wrench might save the day if you snap one. Breaking a pick usually results from torquing it sideways during removal, which is a definite no-no.

When selecting a pick, the droop-angle is important: too shallow and the pick slips; too steep and it's hard to plant. Many tools come with two or more pick options for versatility. On alpine routes, choose drooped or curved picks for climbing and self-arresting. Curved picks penetrate with the natural arc of your swing, but they're not as secure as drooped picks for hooking.

Reverse-curved (re-curved) picks work fine for alpine climbing, but not so well for self-arresting. On water ice, re-curved picks rule, both for planting the pick and hooking. With most re-curved picks, you need a wrist snap at the end of the swing for good penetration. Re-curved picks also seem to work best for dry tooling.

For brittle ice, nothing beats a tube pick, though few manufacturers offer them. On the down side, tube picks clog in slushy ice, don't dry tool well, break easier, and they'll core sample a big chunk out of your rope if you misfire.

Whatever picks you use, keep them sharp for clean penetration. You can sharpen picks with a flat file; for tube picks use a rat-tail file.

### Adze

Adzes come in many styles. The most versatile ones work for chopping ice, planting in rotten ice or hard snow where a pick shears through, and camming in cracks or grabbing edges on mixed climbs. Despite all this utility, some waterfall climbers forgo the adze in favor of two hammers so they can drive pitons and pound-ins with either hand, and to avoid catching an adze in the face if a tool pops. If you use an adze, carry it in your weaker hand, and a hammer in your favored hand for placing pound-ins, pitons, and ice hooks.

### Hammer

It's pretty simple to make a good hammerhead. Make sure the face of the hammer lines up properly with the arc of your swing—some tools with radically bent shafts force you to choke up on the shaft to hammer, which deflates your swing. If you'll be climbing mixed routes, look for a hammerhead designed to be jammed in cracks.

## Grip

The grip is your contact point with the axe. A grippy texture is nice for swinging and hanging from the tool. Molded grips are great—until you try a shaft plant. You can cut the bottom flange off a molded grip to improve performance in alpine situations. Some tool shafts contour to fit your hand, so a molded grip is unnecessary. Most axe shafts are metal, so the grip material should insulate your hand from the heat-sucking metal.

Tennis players have numerous grip diameters to choose from, to perfectly match their hand size. Ice climbers are still waiting for a variable-diameter ice axe shaft. Until one comes along, the diameter of the grip remains important when selecting a tool. Climbers with small hands do better with thin grips.

## Shaft

Shaft shapes vary wildly—with the exception of straight shafts, almost no two are the same. Which shape is best? Straight shafts work best for alpine climbing, because you can plunge them into hard snow. Bent grips (tools with the shaft bent only at the grip) make swinging and holding onto the tools easier on steep ice, prevent some knuckle bashing, and can still be shaft-planted in snow. Bent shafts work great on steep, technical ice, especially for reaching past bulges and around cauliflowers, and they allow a more natural position for your wrists, which relieves stress. However, they can be unstable when dry tooling and are difficult to plunge into hard snow. Choose a shaft for the style of climbing you prefer, and try to test the different shapes to see what you like best.

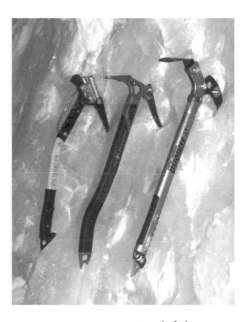

Bent shaft, bent grip, and straight shaft.

## Spike

A simple, sharp spike bites the ice when you're using the axe like a cane for balance. If the spike is too long, or raked forward, it'll strike the ice midswing, foiling your swing. I like spikes with a hole large enough to clip; this is useful when backing up the belay anchors with the axes. The hole also accepts a fifi hook if your leading tactics include hanging to place protection. Keep the spike relatively sharp, but be careful—the spike is the point that loves to shred fabric and skin.

If I'm carrying a third tool, I prefer a short, light hammer with no spike, because a spike dangling from my harness seems likely to rip flesh in a fall, and it's one extra point I can do without.

## Wrist Leash

A detachable leash lets you easily free your hand to place an ice screw, belay, or just rest and warm your hands.

It's bewildering that something as simple as a wrist leash is so rarely well designed. You want a leash that locks securely on your wrist, is easy to exit, and is comfortable to hang from on steep ice. The leash should be strong—wimpy buckles attaching wrist leashes to my tools make me nervous. Easily adjustable leashes are nice for accommodating different glove systems. For alpine situations, the leash must allow you to slide your hand to the head of the axe.

This leash is attached below the head to the axe, and cinched tight around the wrist. The length is adjusted so the hand rests perfectly on the grip, just above the spike.

This leash is attached to the head of the ice axe. However, it is adjusted too short, which inhibits swinging the tool. If the leash is adjusted too long, you have to grip extra hard on steep ice. It's important to get the length just right.

Insert your hand into a twist-in leash, and twist the leash until it's tight enough on your wrist to support your weight. This leash is attached to the axe near the hand loop, which decreases the pump factor on steep ice, but can make it harder to slide your hand to the head of the axe.

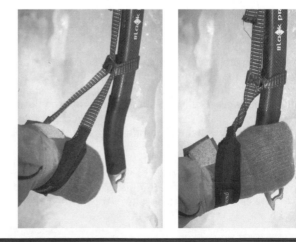

The available leashes present many options: some tighten with plastic buckles or cam-locks, others rely on Velcro, and some require twisting your hand into the sling. The worst have a slider that always creeps up the leash just when you're getting pumped.

Some leashes attach at the head of the tool; when placing protection, or rock climbing with your hands, you can simply let go, and the tool dangles nicely out of the way. With this style of leash, it's easy to move your hand to the head of the axe. Other leashes attach midshaft. A leash that's fastened to the lower part of the shaft provides good hand support, and can decrease the pump on steep ice, but if adjusted poorly, can make it inconvenient to slide your hand to the axe head. Midshaft leashes are also easier to recover to your hand after placing protection. A recent innovation is a leash that detaches from the tool, thereby freeing your hands to place pro.

Experiment with different styles of leashes and tools. It's important to learn what works best for you. If you don't like the leash that came with your tool, buy another one. But don't give up on a leash (or tool) too fast. Most tools and leashes have a learning curve, and you may learn to love a setup that you hated at first, once you adapt to it. Whatever style of wrist leash you choose, keep the length adjusted perfectly, with your little finger sitting just above the spike. A few climbers actually like their little finger to sit on the spike. Some climbers spray water repellent treatment onto their leashes to help prevent them from freezing up.

## Length

The most popular length for waterfall tools is 50 centimeters, although 55 centimeters can be better for large climbers, or those who don't often get on steep terrain. However, 55-centimeter tools are rare. For smaller climbers, 45 centimeters is the length of choice. Forty five–centimeter tools are fairly common, though not every model comes in this length. For snow and low-angle alpine ice, a 60- to 80- centimeter basic axe serves better, with 70 centimeters being the most common length for a basic mountaineering axe.

## Weight

*Picks with and without a head weight.*

Light tools save energy when you're hooking or dry tooling, or when you're carrying them on your pack. They generally penetrate well in alpine or soft water ice, but in hard ice you'll need a snappy swing to plant light tools. Conversely, heavy tools penetrate hard ice well, but sap energy to swing. However, it's more efficient to plant a heavier tool in one or two blows, compared to a featherweight that takes half a dozen swings. The most important consideration about the weight of a tool is balance.

Ideally, most of the weight is in the head, as close to the pick as possible. A heavy shaft, spike, or hammer head can spoil the balance of a tool. Some tools offer optional head weights that improve a tool's balance and add heft to your swing.

### Strength

Based on results of testing that I conducted for *Climbing* magazine in 1997, I would never trust ice tools as the sole anchors in a belay. For normal use, what's more important than strength is durability. All of the tools seem well built, and you'll have your work cut out to trash them. One exception is misfires: if you strike a shaft sharply against the ice, you could bend or break the shaft, especially on carbon fiber models. This isn't likely to happen if you swing accurately. Bent shafts provide clearance to prevent misfires.

## CRAMPONS

With crampons, we can dance on ice and hard snow, but I wouldn't wear them in a bowling alley. Without them, we may as well stay home. Many choices exist when selecting crampons. Choose crampons compatible with the types of ice you'll be climbing.

Rigid crampons—those that do not bend—rule on frozen waterfalls. They are solid, secure and stable, vibrate little, and provide a good platform to stand on. Add vertical front points and a step-in binding and you have the ultimate waterfall crampon. Vertical front points enter the ice cleanly and provide a strong, stable foothold, though they can shear through slushy ice or snow. For soft conditions, horizontal front points provide more surface area, and they still work okay on hard water ice. One design that shares the best of both worlds has vertical front points with horizontal fins to increase surface area when the points are buried.

Step-in bindings add convenience—flip the heel clamps up, fasten the safety straps, and you're good to go. Make sure the bindings have a reliable, tight fit on the boots so the crampons cannot cast off midclimb. Heel bails must close tightly, and the toe bails must properly fit your boot welts. If the toe bail doesn't perfectly follow the contours of your welt, mold it with a hammer until it does (this only works for minor modifications). You can also cut grooves in your plastic boots to make crampons fit better, but I'd be careful here—go too deep and you've trashed your pricey footwear. If the toe bail is mis-sized, another size bail may be available. If you already own your boots, take them into the shop to ensure compatibility when you choose your crampons. If you own your crampons, take them in when you choose your boots. The retail sales staff

1. Front pointing (left) and flat footing with all of the bottom points contacting the ice (right).

2. Horizontal frontpoints (upper) and vertical frontpoints (lower).

should be qualified to ensure that you get what you need. You may also want to bring along an experienced ice climber whose opinion you respect.

Step-in crampons have safety straps so your crampon won't plummet if the binding releases. Metal buckles on the safety straps are more durable than plastic ones. Straps that fasten the toe bail to the safety straps (available on some models of crampons) add security. It's important to make sure your crampons are secure each time you put them on. Losing a crampon mid-pitch will leave you calling for Mr. Wizard to save you.

Strap-on crampons fasten securely to your boots, but my most vivid memory of strap-ons is freezing my fingers while worming the straps through their eyelets, then freezing my toes due to the compression of the straps. The modern strap-ons are better, but still, securely fitting step-ins are far more convenient.

The great debate of modern ice climbers—mono-points versus dual front points—is as polarizing as the liberal versus conservative battles in Washington. Mono advocates insist the single front point is best in every water ice situation. Dual front pointers are equally adamant. I'm a moderate—I've found monos to work great on mixed routes, and sometimes on hard waterfalls. They offer more flexibility than dual points, like slippers compared to stiff rock shoes. With monos you can set your feet lightly in old pick holes, place them precisely on tiny rock edges, divots, and cracks, and rotate the points for moving sideways or back stepping. Monos encourage a fun, rock climbing style on the ice—many top climbers use monos almost exclusively.

Dual front points add stability to your stance, which can mean more security on pure water ice. I remember cringing as I watched a good climber sketching on chandelier ice because his monos kept popping. Two other climbers wearing dual point crampons cruised the same route with nary a foot sketch. With two front points, the added stability can save energy on long routes, and if you break a point off, you still have a fighting chance. And on soft ice, two points are less likely to slice through than one. For new ice climbers, especially those who are not masterful rock technicians, dual points may be the best way to start.

1. Strap-on crampon (lower) and step-in crampon (upper).

2. Lace crampon straps so they run from outside to inside. Set them fairly tight, and finish as shown in the previous photo.

3. Mono and dual front points.

4. A mono point placed on a well-used rock divot.

Whether climbing on monos or duals, good foot technique means seating the second row of points in the ice for stability. With monos this gives you a tripod to stand on, and with duals you'll get the stability of four points. Try both monos and duals for yourself and decide which work best in what conditions. Many crampons can be switched from monos to duals, so you can try both. If you plan to switch often, however, it's far easier to have two pairs of crampons.

The crampon bottom points should be spaced closely enough at the instep (front to back) to prevent the rocker effect on ice humps. Keep all points—front and bottom—sharp, so they bite the ice. Don't power grind them or you can ruin the temper of the metal. File front points mostly on the top edge, and bottom points on the front and back.

For less technical terrain, hinged crampons bend at the instep for easy walking. They can work all right on ice, provided you have rigid boots, but they are less stable than rigids. For snow climbing and glacier walking, flexible boots and hinged crampons fight snowballing, the dangerous phenomenon when wet snow collects in big clumps and obscures the points of your crampons. Crampons with vertical rails—"cookie cutters"—are more prone to snowballing than those with horizontal rails. According to Jojo, "the biggest advance in crampon safety ever has been the anti-balling plates that you can now buy for most models. It should be against the law to sell crampons without them. Get some."

Some climbers like to carry their crampons in a crampon bag to keep them from poking holes in your stuff. Many others attach the crampons outside of the pack, to save the weight and bulk of the crampon bag.

1. Dual front points well-planted in the ice, with the second row also engaged for stability.
2. Some crampons have points on the back for heel hooking.
3. You can make your own heel points by placing wood screws or sheet metal screws in the heel clamps. This is actually a better location for the point than the back of the crampon.

## ICE PROTECTION

Depending on the route, your rack might include ice screws, pound-ins, ice hooks, pitons, wired nuts, and cams. You won't carry all of this stuff on every route—a little research will allow you to pare the rack down to a few necessary pieces. For example, on a big, fat flow, you can leave the rock gear and ice hooks at home.

Modern, high quality screws cut ice like butter, and they cause little disturbance in fragile or brittle conditions. With practice, you'll learn how to fire screws in fast and climb on. The models with a crank handle are the quickest to place and remove. Short screws, also called stubbies, come in handy on thin ice, but they're usually weaker than long screws. If I know the ice is thick, I'll leave the short screws out and bring half medium and half long screws. If I'm not sure, I may toss in a couple stubbies for good measure.

It's sometimes easier for a leader to drive a pound-in, though the second pays dearly because pound-ins are harder to remove. Modern screws work so well that pound-ins have lost popularity. Still, I sometimes carry a couple for desperate "need gear fast" placements in convoluted ice where I can't get a screw in fast. After all, the leader's security always overrides the second's convenience.

For thin ice (3 or 4 inches thick), and frozen dirt, moss, or turf, ice hooks come in handy, though they should never replace an ice screw or pound-in, because they're weaker and less stable.

On a thin or mixed route, or if you have exposed rock, rock protection can be quicker and stronger than ice gear. Pitons can work well in icy cracks, especially angle or Z-shaped pins; nuts and camming units are often essential. Tri-cams sometimes work great in icy cracks—some climbers won't leave home without them. Clipping the protection with quickdraws helps your rope run clean, and minimizes the chance of the rope unclipping if you fall.

To tie off protruding ice screws, and rig natural protection, you'll need some slings. Spectra beats nylon for tie offs because it's more resistant to cutting. A handful of load-limiting quickdraws (Yates Screamers, for example) also comes in handy for reducing the force on your protection if you fall. I often carry a cordelette as well, for rigging anchors, cutting up for rappel slings, and in case I need to perform a self-rescue.

When wearing gloves and mittens, little sport carabiners can be tough to clip. Big shapely carabiners and those with wire gates clip easily. I prefer extra-strong carabiners for ice climbing, because with ice gear I'm running 15 to 20 pounds heavier than on summer rock, and I'm often way above the pro. This is no time to have a carabiner break! Ice protection is covered in more detail in Chapters 6 and 7.

*1. Ice screws come in many dimensions, but you can break them into three basic groups: shorties (for thin ice), medium-length, and long. Here we have 10-, 17-, and 22-centimeter screws. (See Chapter 7 for more on the strength of ice screws.)*

*2. A pound-in can be nice when you're pumped and need pro fast. Since ice screws have become much easier to set, pound-ins have become less popular in the past few years.*

*3. Ice hooks give marginal protection in frozen dirt, moss, and 3- to 4-inch thick ice.*

*4. Rock gear is often quicker to place and more reliable than ice gear, if you can find exposed rock on the route. Rock gear is essential on many mixed routes.*

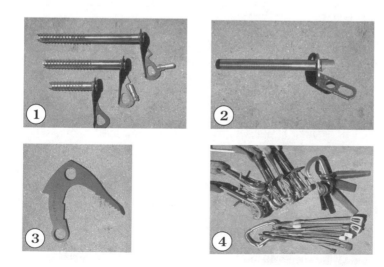

## HARNESS

If you'll be climbing short routes, your standard rock climbing harness can work fine, provided it fits over your layers without constricting movement. For alpine routes, or ice routes in an alpine environment, diaper-style harnesses are convenient. You can put them on over crampons, and when nature calls you can drop the back of the harness without untying. Choose a harness that's easy to buckle when wearing gloves or mittens and bulky clothes. Avoid thick padding, which can absorb water and freeze. Your insulation layers will provide enough padding.

*Two or three hammer holsters attached to your harness or a waist belt give you a place to carry your tools.*

### Holsters

Attach two or three holsters to the harness or a separate belt for slinging your tools. I generally use my harness, but if you use a separate sling instead, you can easily slide them out of the way in chimneys and other tight situations. Make sure the tools fit loosely in the holsters so you can draw like Rooster Cogburn when the rock turns to ice, but not so loose that you lose your precious tools. When you holster your tools, it's a good idea to clip off the wrist leashes to your harness so you can't lose them. If the axe has a large hole in the head, you can clip a carabiner through the hole to another carabiner on your harness racking loops. As Jojo says, "nothing adds piece of mind like a tool you *know* isn't going to go the way of the buffalo." He knows, because one time he was reaching for his third tool after breaking a pick on the Quebec ultraclassic *La Pomme d'Or*, only to realize that the tool had fallen out of his holster and was now resting on a ledge 30 meters below.

## ROPES

Many climbers prefer half ropes (formerly called double ropes) for safety in case a rope gets cut, and to decrease the impact force on ice protection. Double cords give extra protection to inexperienced seconds, who are likely to chop a rope with their ice axes. Often you need two ropes to descend anyway, so you may as well incorporate both ropes into the lead protection.

The standard rope length was 50 meters, but now climbers prefer 60- and even 70-meter cords so they can run longer pitches and avoid uncomfortable belays.

Single ropes can work fine, especially on short routes. Some climbers use a single 100-meter rope for leading ultralong pitches. This tactic saves time by avoiding extra belays, but you need a lot of ice screws; the belayer has to hunker in for a long, chilly vigil, and if the second comes off early in the pitch, they'll take a *super-bungee* fall with all the rope stretch. One friend of mine witnessed a 40-foot whipper when the second came off with such a long cord.

Choose a dry-coated rope that doesn't absorb water and freeze up. Rock climbing on dry ropes wears the dry coating off.

## Minimizing Impact Force

The impact force of a rope is an important specification that should be listed on a rope's hang tag, or mentioned in a magazine rope review. The UIAA specifies that single ropes must subject the climber to less than 2,640 pounds of force in their drop tests. Some ropes generate much less force, as low as 1,500 pounds in the UIAA test; half ropes create less impact force than single ropes, if you clip only one of them into the protection. In a fall, ropes with a low impact force put less force on your protection by stretching more. This reduction in force could make the difference between pro holding or ripping out, but the extra stretch increases your chance of hitting a ledge or the ground. Despite the increased falling distance of a low impact rope, for ice climbing it's best to choose a low impact rope, because ice protection is often sketchy.

## BELAY/RAPPEL DEVICE

Most climbers use a standard rock climbing belay device for belaying and rappeling ice climbs. As a stand-in, it's crucial to know the hip belay and body rappel in case your ropes become hopelessly iced. See *How to Rock Climb* by John Long.

## ALPINE PACK

Take a crag pack and add ice axe loops, crampon straps, a little extra volume, and voilà!—you have a pack for ice climbing. For alpine climbing, add a removable pad for bivis, an extendable lid for overflow, easy-to-operate compression straps, drop-out ice axe tubes, a bomber haul loop, and possibly a bivi extension and gear-racking loops. Other than the lid, avoid external pockets.

Look for a pack with a simple, thoughtful design, a slim profile, and avoid unneeded features. For day climbs, 2,500 to 3,500 cubic inches should meet your volume needs. Multi-day alpine climbs will require more like 4,000 to 4,500 cubic inches. When choosing volume, some climbers go for the smallest pack possible to decrease the load they carry (which often increases the load that their partners haul). This strategy has merit as long as you don't end up lashing things outside the pack. I prefer a pack that easily fits all of my stuff, but just barely.

The suspension distributes weight between your shoulders, hips, and lower back. In an alpine pack, you might sacrifice some comfort for sleekness. Aluminum or plastic stays improve a pack's comfort, but also add bulk and weight that's unnecessary when you're going fast and light. Even with the best suspension and all the straps tightened, a pack won't carry well if it's not loaded properly. When packing, balance the load between left and right. Put heavy gear near the center of your back, with enough padding to keep the rack from digging into your back. Pack the load tight, then cinch the compression straps.

Before you buy a pack, make sure it fits. Load the pack up to carrying weight, adjust the straps, and test it out. The weight test gives you an idea of comfort and fit, but in the end, there's nothing like humping the pack fully loaded for a few miles to learn how it works. Females may find the best fit in a pack designed for women.

## DRESSING FOR SUCCESS

### Boots

Good boots are essential to ice climbing success and enjoyment. You have two choices: leather or plastic. For extreme cold, or climbers who easily get cold feet, plastic double boots are the ticket. They're warm, comfortable, waterproof, low-maintenance, and protective. You can also remove the inner boots for drying, or lounging around camp.

If temperatures are not frigid, sturdy leather boots work great. They're lighter, easier to walk in, more comfortable, and they out-climb double boots. The improved ankle flexibility facilitates French technique, and the lighter, smaller size suits hard mixed climbing. Leather boots must be treated occasionally to keep the leather supple and waterproof.

*1. Plastic boots are standard for climbing in cold conditions.*

*2. Leather boots are lighter, more comfortable, and provide more sensitivity.*

These days, most serious alpinist/ice climbers have both types of boots. If you can have only one pair, though, pick double boots because they'll work in any conditions. Whatever you select, find a good fit. Boots fitted too tight impede circulation and cause cold feet; too big and your feet slosh around. When sizing boots, put on all the socks that you'll wear climbing.

For multi-day adventures, a vapor barrier keeps your socks and boots dry, and your feet warm. First put on a thin sock, then a vapor barrier, then a thick, insulating sock. The vapor barrier can be a coated nylon store-bought model, or simply a bread bag. When using a vapor barrier, it's essential to dry your socks and feet out every night to avoid trench foot.

You can also get neoprene socks, which offer insulation and serve as a vapor barrier. You might wear a thin liner sock inside the neoprene, or wear the neoprene directly, with an insulating sock over it. When using neoprene, remember to dry your feet out every night.

Custom foot inserts distribute the pressure on your feet, rather than allowing "hot spots" to develop. They'll add a lot of comfort to your abused feet on long days out.

## Fit to be Tried—Finding the Perfect Boot.

*by* Joe Josephson

Fit is the most important factor when choosing a boot. Find a retailer experienced in fitting boots, with a large inventory so you can try several models. When fitting boots, lace them while bearing weight on your foot. Try many models—remember, the sales staff works for you. If you can't find a good fit, look elsewhere for other brands and models. Patience is the key.

Choose boots that will serve in the temperature range you climb in. If your feet get cold, Supergaiters can help, but really, you need a warmer boot.

With plastic boots, the biggest problem is that people often buy them too big. The key is shell sizing, which is problematic because manufacturers offer only one shell size to accommodate several liner sizes. First find the proper shell size. Wearing your normal climbing socks with no liner, press your toes against the front of the boot. Ideally, you should have about an inch of space in the heel. Too much space and your toes will slam into the toe box pitch after pitch. Once you have the right shell, find a liner that fits the shell and your foot.

With single boots, focus on the fit of the toes. Any binding or pressure here will cause cold feet. Heel lift should be minimal, but you can cure some lift with custom foot beds.

After purchasing boots, unless you were lucky enough to find the exact fit, take them to an expert follow-up fitter for customizing, especially if you have bunions and/or old injuries. A good fitter can work wonders modifying boots to fit your feet perfectly. I've seen climbers with destroyed ankles climb again comfortably with customized boots. You can also have thermo-foam liners molded to fit your foot and boot perfectly. They provide the ultimate in warmth, comfort, dryness, fit, and performance.

Through perseverance you will find the boot that works. Once you find that magic slipper, don't even look at the price tag. If you compromise on fit to save cash, your feet will extract every buck you saved—with interest.

## Shell

Shell garments—parkas, anoraks, pants, bibs, one-piece suits, and gaiters—stand as your front-line defense against the elements. Your shell must shed wind, water, and snow to maintain a warm, dry climate inside. If it fails, you could be in trouble.

In extreme environments, the best shell gear is made of waterproof/breathable fabric, which keeps weather out and allows sweat to escape. Many choices exist in this category. You can pick a light, simple design to minimize weight and bulk. For extended use, though, durable fabric and reinforced patches help prevent your razor-sharp ice tools from slicing your garments to shreds.

A parka or anorak combined with pants or bibs works well. Test the fit with your insulation layers before buying. Lift your arms above your head, raise your knees to your chest, and do some squats. Is the shell too tight, does it bind anywhere?

Articulation in the elbows and knees helps here. Do the sleeves stay around your wrists, or do they slide halfway to your elbows? Does the bottom of the jacket lift above your pants? Put on the hood and turn your head. Does the hood turn with you, or do you stare into it? Does the hood work over your climbing helmet?

Look for quality construction. Color may or may not be important to you, but dark clothing offers no visibility at night or in a storm. Is the jacket well ventilated? Easy-to-use pit zips help keep you cool on strenuous approaches.

Pants and bibs should be even more durable than your top. They should allow you to answer nature's calls with ease, and be easy to put on and remove. Full side zips help, especially when you're wearing crampons, snowshoes or skis. For long-term abuse, reinforced knees, seat, and instep combat premature wear. A crampon patch helps, but the only thing that saves pants from sharp crampons is gaiters.

Shell pants are lighter and more compact than bibs, but offer less protection and pocket space. One of my all-time beefs with pants or bibs is this: I'm carrying a heavy load, and buttons or zippers on the pants are gouging my hips. Try the pants on with a heavy pack, to check for nasty pressure points. Can you ventilate the pants, even with your pack on? The downside of some shell pants is that the slick pants are bad for leg hooks and knee-barring across an icy chimney, and if you fall on snow, you'll accelerate like a luge.

Many climbers forgo the shell on their legs, instead choosing a pant made of woven stretch fabric that is wind and water resistant. This style of pants offers superb freedom of movement on the approach and the climb.

*A one-piece shell gives stout protection against evil weather and dripping waterfalls, but the high price is a painful deterrent.*

For the ultimate protection, a one-piece suit is warm, efficient and stylish. It's also expensive—you'll shed tears when you punch that first hole in the suit. A one-piece is lighter and warmer than a parka/pant combination, and gives better freedom of movement. Best of all, you never get snow down the back of your pants.

Gaiters keep snow out of your boots, confine your boot laces so you don't trip on them, and protect your pricey suit from razor-sharp crampons. Gaiters that fasten in front with a wide strip of Velcro are the easiest on and off. Super-gaiters, those that insulate down to the welt of your boot, add significant warmth to a boot.

After hard use, the water-repellent coating wears off of shell fabric, allowing the garment to "wet out". You can restore the repellency by treating the shell with the available chemical sprays.

## Insulation

While the shell keeps wind and moisture out, insulation layers keep heat in. What insulation to wear obviously depends on the temperature, and how active you'll be. Wear too many layers and you'll heat up like a 100-watt light bulb once you get moving; too few layers and you'll shiver at every belay. For normal ice climbing temperatures, medium-weight fleece pants, and a light synthetic shirt coupled with a fleece jacket should do the trick. For a slightly warmer ensemble, wear thicker pants or bibs, and add a fleece vest or extra shirt. Make sure the shirt and/or jacket insulates your neck. Cotton is a no-no, because it loses heat when wet, and dries slowly. Wool is okay; it insulates when wet, but it's slow to dry, and makes you smell like a sheep. The best insulation fabrics are the synthetics: polyester, polypropylene, and a host of high-tech derivatives that insulate when wet and wick away water.

*The Negator—nothing can save your morale on those long, frigid belays like a beefy, insulated parka with a hood, and a pair of warm, dry mittens.*

Carry a down parka or vest for belaying and you can skimp on the layers. To minimize weight carry one parka for a team of two climbers—whoever's belaying the leader gets to wear it. If you have a forced bivi, you'll stay warm brawling over who gets the parka. A hood on the parka adds much warmth for little extra weight. In frigid temperatures, the down parka will easily become your favorite piece of gear.

A bare head dumps loads of heat—some claim that up to 50 percent of your heat loss comes from the head. A warm hat that fits under your helmet is

---

### Clues about Clothing

*by* Joe Josephson

One crux of ice climbing is overcoming the psychological damage inflicted by spending all day getting cold, wet, and mortally frightened. This is where preparation comes into play. Efficient climbing is largely about having your systems dialed.

Avoid sweating on the approach. Strip off layers, ventilate, and adjust your pace to avoid soaking your clothes. No shell venting system will keep you dry if you're postholing uphill like an elk in wolf country.

I almost always carry "The Negator"—a large insulated coat that fits over everything. The Negator tames the cold, wet, windy environment of ice climbing. Down insulation works, provided you dry it out each night, but synthetic insulations work better.

Lace your boots while you're standing and bearing weight. Otherwise, you'll get the laces too tight and wonder why your $400 expedition boots don't work.

If you loathe climbing with a pack, a convenient place to stash extra gloves is inside your gaiters. Another option is to clip the detachable lid of your pack to your harness.

essential. For anything but roadside cragging, carry two hats for extra warmth at the belays, and in case you lose one (or maybe one extra per team if you're trying to shave grams).

Don't skimp on clothing—it's perhaps your most important outdoor gear!

### Gloves and Mittens

Gloves beat mittens for climbing, especially for placing and clipping pro; but mittens are warmer. I like to have a pair of each. I'll climb with gloves, and if it's cold, belay with mittens, keeping the gloves in my jacket so they don't freeze. For gloves and mitts, I prefer models with a thick pile liner protected by a waterproof/breathable, durable shell. Some folks wear mitts or gloves equipped with keeper leashes (like you had in kindergarten). They place gear and clip barehanded (or with a thin liner glove) while the mitt hangs from their wrist. This system has one downfall, as the mitts tend to collect ice chips while they dangle.

It's nice if your gloves and mittens are "waterproof." Waterproof or not, they tend to get wet, though the models with seamless waterproof/breathable inserts stay fairly dry. You can stretch the temperature limits of gloves or mittens by inserting chemical heat packs (be sure to keep them dry). On *Wowie Zowie* in Valdez, Alaska, a 500-foot monster that started off with rotten ice and finished with overhanging icicles, my partner Rodrigo Mujica pooh-poohed my heat packs. Later, Rodrigo, who

*A good pair of waterproof gloves helps keep your hands warm and dry.*

is a distinguished high mountain guide, was singing their praises after we got soaked to the bone and he had to belay the second 250-foot WI6 pitch with the mercury hovering at 10 degrees F.

For mixed climbing in reasonably warm conditions, a thin pair of liner gloves will protect your hands somewhat, and allow good dexterity. Make sure your gloves have a clean design around the wrist, to avoid pressure points from your wrist leash.

### Eye Protection

Durable sunglasses are essential for protecting your eyes from the ultraviolet rays of the sun, as well as from flying pieces of ice. When I'm not wearing eye protection, I close my eyes at the instant that the pick strikes the ice.

People who wear prescription glasses should consider using contact lenses and non-prescription sunglasses. If your sunglasses fog and you have to remove them, you can still focus.

## Accessories

Depending on the duration, approach, terrain, and the likelihood of extreme weather, you should include the following items in your pack:
• sunscreen (SPF 30 or higher, essential in sunny weather)
• facemask (for cold, windy weather)
• goggles (if heavy snowfall or blowing snow is possible, especially with frigid temperatures, or ski approaches)
• headlamp with spare bulb and batteries (indispensable for early starts, late descents, and multi-pitch routes)
• first-aid kit (the more remote your trip, the bigger the kit)
• small pocket knife (for cutting rappel slings, though a pick or adze will do in a pinch)
• multi-tool (for various repairs on multi-day trips, or ski approaches)
• map and compass (unless the approach is short and simple)
• shovel (essential for travel in avalanche terrain—one for each climber)
• avalanche beacon (one per climber. Essential in avalanche terrain—know how to use it)
• energy food (easy to digest, high-energy food that doesn't easily freeze)
• insulated water bottle (stay hydrated for optimal performance and resistance to cold)
• thermos (there's nothing like a hot, tasty drink on a long, cold belay)
• file (for retuning tools on long mixed routes)
• spare pick with tools (in case you break one)
• heat packs (to keep your hands warm—a large pack inside the boot on the shin helps keep your feet warm in extreme cold)

## Handwear Systems that Work

*by* Joe Josephson

If you climb ice, occasional cold fingers are unavoidable—no one I know has avoided the anguish of rewarming frozen fingers, a painful ritual we call the "screaming barfies." The worst part is enduring the howling laughs of your partners as you moan like Frankenstein.

The trick is to keep cold fingers to an occasional occurrence. To this end, I routinely wear lightweight, durable gloves for the approach. When I reach the climb, these are usually soaked, so I shove them in the pack and bring out a warmer, thicker pair for climbing. I keep in reserve a third pair: superthick, warm mittens, kept dry in the pack for belays; or Formula-One (top-notch) rigs saved for the horror-show pitch, where warm, dry gloves definitely improve the psyche.

Mittens are warmer than gloves, hands down. Climbing in the Canadian Rockies where folks light fires under their engines to thaw their cars, I use mitts for *all* my midwinter climbing. I commonly use wool Dachstein mitts with the cheapest Gore-Tex shell I can find, because I trash two or three shells a season. A bread sack between the mitten and the shell helps on wet routes. Many climbers add foam here, both for protection from bashing and insulation from the ice. For improved performance, frequently waterproof the shells, wax the leather, and seal every seam.

These days gloves are often adequate, thanks to El Niño, new technology, heat packs, and avoiding climbing when it's -40 degrees F. Yet if you have cold hands, are going to altitude or into arctic conditions, mitts are still the ticket. With a little practice you crimp rock holds and clip your rope fast while wearing mittens.

Experimenting to find the glove or mitt that works best is worth the effort. The less you have to worry about keeping your digits, the more you can focus and enjoy climbing your neighborhood horror show.

## STAYING WARM

Belaying an ice pitch can be less than pleasant. You're dodging falling chunks of ice and growing colder by the minute. When you finally climb, it can take half a pitch to warm up. To stay warm at the belay, contract and relax your muscles, and dance around (don't step on the rope). Heat packs, a down jacket, and a thermos full of hot liquid can add physical and psychological comfort at the belay. Staying hydrated is essential—pound liquids before the day starts, and keep drinking throughout the day. If your urine is bright yellow, you're dehydrated, which undermines your athletic performance, promotes frostbite, and lessens your body's ability to cope with altitude.

Cold fingers are the curse of ice climbing. You get chilled belaying, then jump on the ice with hands above your head, pressed against the ice, and constricted by wrist loops. Twenty feet up your hands freeze, and yow!, the pain when they thaw—I've seen seasoned alpinists shed tears. To help prevent cold hands, move around at the belay, windmill your arms to centrifuge blood to the fingers, and avoid caffeine, which constricts blood vessels. Also, limit your intake of alcohol the day before the climb (and certainly don't drink the day of the climb!), because it dilates your peripheral blood vessels, shuttling blood from your core to your extremities, where it cools down and increases your susceptibility to hypothermia. If I've endured a long belay on the ground, I'll sometimes dash 100 meters downhill, then back up, to get my blood flowing and (hopefully) prevent frozen hands.

### Food for Thought

*by* Joe Josephson

Many ice climbing weekends are borne from drunken bravado on Friday night. Chicken wings and stout may provide motivation, but they offer little real fuel for ice climbing. During an arctic front, neither does a low-fat, weight-watching diet. But if you can't stomach the prospect of greasy bratwurst and a liter of olive oil in your spaghetti, there are a few easy "additives" to improve circulation and get an octane boost.

Energy bars and electrolyte drinks provide fast, easy-to-digest energy. Countless varieties exist. My favorite are the gels that squeeze directly into the mouth, because they quickly boost my blood sugar, and they don't freeze.

Short on cash for fancy energy bars? Stick with standard chocolate bars. Skor are my favorite because they pack the most calories per weight.

A thermos of hot tea takes the edge off cold days and endears your compadres after they froze, lashed to the belay while you battled a hard pitch.

Ginger is a good extremity circulatory dilator. Lots of fresh ginger in your food, supplements, or ginger tea in your thermos are good sources.

Cayenne pepper supplements give the most powerful circulatory boost. They may cause stomach discomfort for some, but most get used to it.

# Alpine Ice

*by* Kennan Harvey

In 1913, Conrad Kain guided two clients to the summit of Mount Robson, the highest peak in the Canadian Rockies. Displaying legendary vision and stamina, Kain cut hundreds of footholds up the 700-foot, 50 degree headwall. Countless more steps led to the summit, where Kain turned and said, "Gentlemen, that's as far as I can take you." He might has well have been on the moon. Few, if any, ice climbs of this magnitude had been completed in North America by this time.

*Jack Tackle doing the alpine approach on the West Face of Fitzroy, Patagonia.*

JOE JOSEPHSON PHOTO

Kain's route is now the standard way up Mount Robson. Competent parties armed with modern gear stroll up the headwall in less than an hour. Ironically, most climbers would be unable and unwilling to repeat the Kain route as he first climbed it—go cut 50 steps with an ice axe and you'll see my point. Besides his amazing tenacity, Kain had mastered the principles of low-angle snow and ice climbing—balance, pace, routine, and rhythm. Even with modern equipment, these principles are essential for moving confidently on alpine ice.

This chapter covers the basics of snow and alpine ice climbing. From here you can don crampons and ice axes and cruise moderate alpine ice routes, or just approach and descend from waterfalls. But start off slowly. On my first day wearing crampons, I skewered my calf and launched headfirst down a 40-degree slope, landing on my partner. Luckily we were at the bottom of the slope.

## ALPINE ICE EQUIPMENT

*Two ways to hold the axe—take your choice.*

For mountaineering and easy alpine ice, choose a standard, 60- to 80- centimeter ice axe. I'm 5'11", and I use a 70-centimeter axe. On steeper alpine ice climbs I use straight-shafted technical tools, 50 to 55 centimeters long.

A leash prevents dropping your axe, and gives a clip-in point if you bury the axe as an anchor. Choose a leash that's easy to get in and out of, since you'll be switching hands with each change of direction. On steeper ice, twist the leash around your wrist to cinch it tight.

When climbing with one axe, hold it in your uphill hand. I loop my thumb under the adze and circle my fingers around the pick, so I'm ready to execute a self-arrest. Many climbers do the opposite, with fingers under the adze, which is more comfortable. Take your pick.

For alpine climbing, the leather boots and rigid crampons described in Chapter 2 work perfectly. In cold temperatures, go with plastic double boots. For the summer mountaineer, flexible, strap-on crampons work fine—they're less expensive, lighter and work on light footwear in less technical situations. I've even strapped flexible crampons onto hiking shoes, but a waterproof leather boot works best.

Whatever style of crampon you choose, they're all lethally sharp. Use gaiters to keep your pant legs from flapping, catching your crampons and tripping you, as mine did on my first ice climb. Walk slightly bow-legged until you develop a natural rhythm. Beware of wet snow balling up in your crampons—anti-balling plates are a great investment in safety. If you don't have them, smack your crampon with an axe to clear the snow. In bad conditions, you may have to do this with every step, or you might do better to remove the crampons, if the terrain allows.

# SNOW

Snow is incredibly diverse and complex—it runs the gamut from bottomless sugar snow that's nearly impossible to travel through, to breakable crust that supports your weight one step, then breaks through the next step, to hard-packed, cruiser snow that makes approaches and climbing easy. Sometimes you'll experience all three conditions in a few hundred meters. Generally speaking, the more you learn, the less you blindly trust snow stability. You could devote a whole book to the intricacies of snow climbing, but we're keeping it simple here.

Snow can kill, especially when it's fresh or wet. It falls fast and furious and removes everything in its path. Before launching into the alpine world, learn about avalanche safety. Neglecting this is foolish, because avalanches kill more ice climbers and skiers than all other hazards combined. Always be prepared to bail if conditions are not safe.

Sometimes, you'll take a calculated risk, traveling through a zone of objective hazard that you've deemed *safe enough*. With good technique you'll move quickly through these zones, so practice these techniques to perfection.

For further reading about avalanche safety, see the Appendix.

## Kicking Steps

Kicking steps is useful on low-angle, soft snow when crampons are not necessary. You can kick steps with just a pair of leather boots (and hopefully an ice axe in case you slip). Kicking steps is pretty simple—you wind up and kick the snow until you've created a step. It may take one kick in soft snow, or several in harder snow. Also look for natural flat spots or lodged stones where no kicks are required. Stand up straight—if you lean in, you might blow out the foot platform and slip.

The position of greatest balance, the *rest stance*, is with your uphill leg out front, slightly bent, and the downhill leg straight, supporting most of your body weight. The steeper you attack the

*Kicking steps on an easy, soft snow slope. No crampons are necessary here.*

slope, the more pronounced the rest stance becomes. From the rest stance, step the trailing foot forward and uphill, crossing your legs, then step back to the rest stance. The key to endurance is pacing yourself—remember, the tortoise beats the hare every time. To really conserve energy, take a slight pause at each rest stance. If the terrain is exposed, you should carry an ice axe, and use it like a cane for balance. Advance the axe from the rest stance: "step, step, move the axe, repeat."

The rest stance.

To diagonal up the slope, step through, crossing the legs. This is the out-of-balance position.

Then step back to the rest stance, with the lower leg straight, supporting most of your weight. Now move the axe up.

## Marching on a Z

On a snow slope you'll often switchback up the easiest terrain. Kick steps diagonally up the slope, and when you're ready to switchback, turn the uphill foot in the new direction and kick a good step. Now your feet are splayed like a duck. Follow with the trailing foot, back to the rest stance.

If you have an axe, use it for balance: plant the spike firmly in the snow, change directions with the uphill foot, switch the axe to the new uphill hand, and finish the turn. If the snow is hard and steep in places, chop steps with the ice axe. If you have to chop many steps, though, you'll wish for crampons.

The switchbacking routine may feel slow at first, but in the long haul, it saves energy over blasting straight up the slope. Experienced alpinists save energy wherever they can.

*Kick a nice foothold.*

*Turn the uphill foot in the new direction, and switch hands on the axe.*

*Step through in the new direction, with the uphill hand on the axe.*

## Duck Walk

Occasionally on low-angle snow or soft ice I splay my feet out like a duck to relieve my ankles, with my knees wide so all the crampon points penetrate. Turnout flexibility helps here. I use the axe for balance, and the routine goes "step, step, move axe, repeat." Sometimes I place both hands on the head of the axe, and sometimes just one. I seldom use this technique for very long, since it's awkward and it hurts the ankles after a while.

## Descending

Going up is only half of any mountain climb; for any climb to be successful, you have to get back down. If it's not too steep, descending snow requires much less effort than ascending it, because gravity is in your favor. The trick is to descend in control.

1. Glissading is a quick way to descend snow slopes. Keep your axe ready to arrest a fall should you slip.

2. The otter slide, which is basically a sitting glissade, is often the most fun part of the day.

3. The sitting glissade is less elegant but safer than the standing glissade—provided there aren't rocks in the snow.

① ② ③

The plunge step. Keep your leg straight and drive your heel into the snow to create a good foothold.

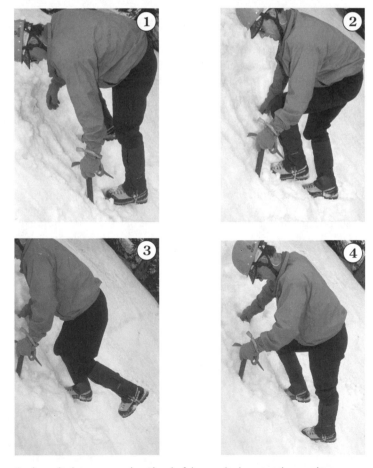

To downclimb, you can plant the shaft low and take several steps down before replanting it.

For fun, speedy, and almost effortless descents, glissading rules. The sitting glissade is the most secure. Remove your crampons (provided it's safe to do so), because if you snag them while sliding, you could snap your ankle or start tumbling. Sit facing downhill and dig in your heels. Hold the axe across your body and slide down the slope. Dig the spike and your heels into the snow to control your speed. Lift your butt off the snow if you see any rocks coming.

The standing glissade is more stylish *and* more difficult, especially with a heavy pack. Basically, you ski down on your boots—the better your skiing skills, the easier you'll find glissading. Bend your knees into a semicrouch, and keep the axe ready to self-arrest if you lose control. Face the fall line and point your toes downhill to accelerate, swivel your hips and edge the boots sideways to turn and slow down. Link turns like a slalom skier to control your speed. To stop quickly, throw a side skid and dig in hard. Failing that, you can drop into a self-arrest. Once you master glissading, you can confidently cruise down moderate snow slopes.

If glissading won't work, try plunge-stepping. Walk straight down the slope, using the axe like a cane. When stepping, keep your leg straight and use your weight to plunge the heel aggressively into the snow to create a deep step.

If it's too steep to walk down, turn sideways, or face the slope and downclimb. You can plunge the shaft or pick of the axe into the snow for security.

## Snow Anchors

When belaying on snow, find rock anchors if possible. Barring that, you can use T-shaped snow pickets, snow flukes, buried ice axes or packs, or a bollard cut into the snow. For all of these, the firmness of the snow will determine how strong the anchor is. Luckily, snow slopes are usually less than vertical, so the force on your anchors is considerably less than on vertical terrain. In very firm snow, pickets provide a fast, strong anchor. Just pound them into the snow, angled back about 45 degrees from the direction of pull. Two pickets placed in series, one above the other, or placed side by side and equalized, makes a belay anchor. It's important that the clipping sling on the picket is right at the snow level.

In slightly less firm snow, snow flukes, also called deadmen, can be driven into the snow. Bury them at 45 degrees to the slope angle, and cut a slot for the cable to rest in. The idea is that when loaded, the fluke will dig itself deeper into the snow to stop a fall. This works okay if the snow is consistently firm, but if the fluke hits a soft spot, or a hard spot, it may be deflected out of the snow. If you don't have deadmen or pickets, you can girth hitch a sling midshaft on an ice axe, then bury the ice axe sideways in the snow. Be sure to cut a slot for the sling to run through, then stomp snow firmly on top of the axe. You can also sling and bury a pack in the same fashion.

With some labor, you can also build a bollard in the snow— you basically dig a trough around a clump of snow, effectively creating a squat snow mushroom to run your rope around. The

Snow picket.

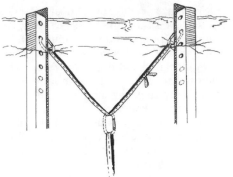

Equalized snow picket. (Ideally the sling should be longer than shown in this illustration, to decrease the angle between the strands of webbing.)

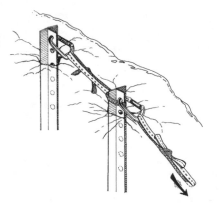

Snow pickets in series.

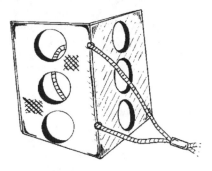

A snow fluke.

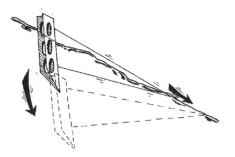

The fluke should be placed about 45 degrees to the slope.

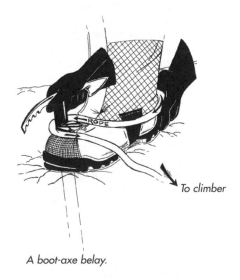

To climber

A boot-axe belay.

softer the snow, the larger the bollard must be—up to several feet wide, and a couple of feet deep. You can drastically increase the strength of a bollard by padding the top edge with a jacket or foam pad, so the rope cannot cut through. Prusik this padding to your rappel rope to retrieve it when you pull the ropes.

A boot-axe belay can be used for a makeshift toprope belay in hard snow. Stomp out a platform in the snow, then drive the axe shaft to the hilt with the pick pointing sideways. Set your boot firmly in the snow, just below the axe. The other foot goes below, in a firm foothold, with the leg straight for bracing against a fall. Run the rope over your boot, around the axe shaft, then around your ankle. Belay with the rope in your downhill hand and weight the axe with a stiff upper arm to hold it in place. The upper hand also takes in rope as the climber moves. The boot-axe belay is not that strong, so use it accordingly.

## Self-Arrest

If you slip on a snow slope, a quick self-arrest will stop your fall—and possibly save your life. It's important to have the self-arrest techniques dialed, so you can stop fast, before you accelerate out of control. Fortunately it's fun to practice. I've instructed many snow schools at 11,000 feet where beginners log a couple thousand vertical feet of sliding before collapsing in blissful exhaustion. Self-arresting does *not* work on ice.

A spring or summer snow slope is a good place to practice since the snow is slippery and consistently hard. Look for an angle between 30 and 40 degrees with a safe runout below in case you botch a lesson. Barring that, make a J-line for safety: anchor a rope at the top, and again 100 feet down and 20 feet to the side of the upper anchor. Leave the rope slack so it forms a J, and clip the rope with a long sling girth hitched to your harness (use a locking carabiner). Dig out a "launching" platform at the top. Bring waterproof clothing, but wear only fleece on your first attempts (weather allowing), because it will slow your speed somewhat (with slick shell gear on you'll accelerate much faster). For safety, pad the adze on your axe (it will be pointing at your face when you self-arrest), and never practice while wearing crampons—you might catch the points and get flipped. In the

*If you slip, you may be able to drive the shaft into the snow before you start sliding.*

*But never let go of the axe!*

BAD. Don't try to roll toward the spike, or it will jam in the snow and get pulled away from you.

real world, of course, you may be wearing both shell gear and crampons when you need to make a self-arrest, so keep that in mind.

You can fall and slide four different ways: 1) feet first, belly down; 2) feet first, belly up; 3) head first, belly down; and 4) the worst—head first, belly up. A self-arrest technique sequence exists for each falling position. Often, though, if you slip and the snow is soft enough, you can avoid a fancy self-arrest by quickly planting the shaft.

The first rule of self-arrest is *never let go of your axe*. Without the axe, even if it's leashed to your hand, you'll accelerate out of control quicker than you can say *"adiós."*

The easiest position to arrest from is *feet first, belly down*. As you fall, grab the bottom of the axe with your free hand, and pull it diagonally across your chest, with the axe head near your shoulder. If you're holding the axe with your fingers under the adze, quickly reverse your hand on the axe head, so the pick points away from you. Push the pick into the snow, with the spike elevated a few inches, and hang on tight. Arch your back so your chest weights the axe, and dig your toes in, with your feet spread for stability. If you're wearing crampons, hold your feet in the air so they don't snag, and dig your knees in.

Be careful not to brake *too* fast, or the axe may get pulled away from your chest. If this happens, stay calm and quickly get back in position. From the other falling positions, the goal is to twist and turn until you're in the *feet first, belly down* position, then arrest as described above. Falling *feet first, belly up* is like going down a playground slide. To stop, quickly roll over toward the axe head, and finish the self-arrest as above.

Falling *head first, belly down* is intimidating because you're sliding face first down the snow. After you fall, grab the spike and hold the axe with both hands in front of your head. Twist the pick into the snow, to rotate your body to the feet first position. You

If you slip, pull the axe across your chest and drive the pick into the snow. This is the classic self-arrest position, with the back arched so the chest is pushing the axe into the snow, and both feet digging into the snow. If you're wearing crampons, keep your feet in the air and your knees on the snow so you don't catch your front points and get flipped backward.

can hasten the rotation by curving your body slightly. If the pick catches hard the axe might smack your face, so keep your arms straight and look away from the axe. Once your feet are in front, execute the standard self-arrest.

Falling *head first, belly up*, you'll be staring at the sky with your head leading the way—not a comforting position. When practicing, have someone hold your legs on the starting platform, and visualize the sequence before sliding. When you start sliding, quickly sit up and dig the spike into the snow near your waist to swing your body around. As your feet rotate, twist your hips and shoulders toward the snow, until you're in the standard arrest position.

In the worst-case scenario, a tumbling fall, spread your arms and legs to stop the tumbling, then crank the self-arrest from whatever position you end up in. Your success with a critical self-

Oops!

Think fast before you accelerate out of control . . .

. . . roll toward the head of the axe . . .

. . . into the self-arrest position.

*Whoa!*

*Sliding face first down the slope.*

*Hold the axe in front of your head and twist the pick into the snow.*

*This will twist your body around into the self-arrest position.*

arrest depends on the speed with which you initiate the arrest, and your *determination*. Do it fast! If you lose the axe (or don't have one), use your elbows and toes. If your partner falls while roped to you, drop into the self-arrest position and hold tight in case they blow it and can't stop themselves. The self-arrest is your most reliable snow self-belay; even more important is climbing in control, so you never have to self-arrest.

## ALPINE ICE

Many techniques for climbing ice are similar to those for climbing snow, but hard, slippery ice requires more precision and refined technique. Because ice is strong, your points need barely penetrate for good purchase.

### French Technique

The main premise of French technique is keeping both feet flat on the ice, with all bottom points penetrating, to save strain on the calves. I use it to diagonal up slopes, or go straight up, on angles up to 45 degrees. When diagonaling, it's similar to marching on a Z as described on page 42—you switchback your way up the slope. When climbing straight up, you advance the lower foot straight above the higher foot, crossing your legs, then move back to the rest stance.

As the terrain steepens, I point my toes more downward, so I can flex my ankles enough to get all the points in the ice. On the steepest angles, it's like you're leading with your heels. It's important to stomp the points into the ice so they bite—the harder the ice, the harder you must stomp. Leather boots work best for long sessions of French technique, because they allow the ankle to flex. French technique works well for climbing or descending snow or soft ice, but has limited value on waterfall ice.

Ascending with French technique, keeping all the bottom points in contact with the ice.

Descending with French technique.

You can rest by sitting on one of your feet when climbing or descending with French technique.

Plastic boots provide great ankle support for front pointing, which is fast and secure on harder ice and steeper angles. Plastic boots limit French technique to use on moderate angled snow and alpine ice, since it's hard to flex them. Still, it's valuable to master French technique, because it's ultraefficient for climbing long, moderate slopes, and on steeper slopes it complements front pointing.

### Three and Nine o'clock

When the angle gets so steep that I can't use pure French technique, I'll front point one foot, keeping the heel low, and flat foot the other. Imagining the face of a clock, the flat foot points toward three or nine, while the front points face twelve. I alternate which foot splays out, while some climbers favor one direction.

As the angle kicks up, you'll use two tools rather than one. On soft ice and hard snow around 50 degrees to 60 degrees, holding the head of the axe and stabbing the picks in like a dagger makes for speedy climbing. On harder ice you'll set the picks for purchase—Chapter 4 thoroughly covers steep-ice technique.

### Front Pointing

On steep alpine *or* waterfall ice, both feet front point most of the time. See Chapter 4 for coverage of this technique.

Practice all of the above techniques, and learn to fluently switch between them as the terrain changes. Stay flexible in your style—mixing up techniques switches muscle groups, so you can "rest" without stopping.

The 3:00 foot position, with the pick set as a handhold.

The 9:00 foot position, with the pick stabbed into the snow like a dagger.

You can cruise up hard snow and soft ice slopes around 50 to 60 degrees by stabbing the picks in like daggers.

Climb smart. While these techniques may be basic, safe decision making in the alpine world is not. Consider the kitten who scampers playfully up a tree, then discovers it doesn't know how get down. Like good wine, proper judgment requires time and preparation.

Aside from technique, alpine climbing requires knowledge of Mother Nature—no technology or climbing prowess can save us from all her furies. And unfortunately, there is no easy way to teach or learn "mountain sense." Always follow your gut feelings, and keep your eyes and mind actively searching for hazards.

### Roping Up

If you rope up, your partner and self-arrest skills are not a reliable belay. A running belay, with two or more pieces of protection between climbers, allows you to safely move simultaneously. Several avoidable tragedies have occurred when an unanchored rope team fell and swept other teams to their deaths. The only time to be roped together without pro is on a low-angle, crevassed glacier. Be especially cautious when descending towards steeper terrain—the consequences for falling may be severe.

### Navigating and Route Finding

It is really important to know your compass directions at all times. Pay attention to the path of the sun, moon, stars, and prevailing wind, since they are helpful direction indicators. Learn how to use a compass, map and altimeter, and trust them. In Canada's Coast Range, we navigated across a 25-mile glacial plateau in a blinding whiteout, arriving within 100 yards of our cache.

Draw a topo of your route using binoculars if possible. Use memory games to remember key landmarks. If you'll be descending the route, look down often, to record visual landmarks as they'll appear on the return.

### Fast and Light

On Mount Huntington in Alaska, my partner and I paused after climbing for two hours. The first ascent team had required 20 days to reach this point. Sold! With fast and light climbing you can wait for the perfect conditions. Your margin for error is small, though. Strong team fitness is essential so you can move fast, as is carrying only essential gear. The limits of speed have hardly been pushed. Got to train to keep up!

May miles of neve carry you to grand views and lofty dreams.

# CHAPTER 4

# Water Ice Technique

*"He who hesitates becomes frost."*

On the ice, attitude is everything. If you think ice climbing is scary, insecure, and dangerous, then it is. But with confidence and technique, standard ice climbs can be a cruise.

## HOW TO PRACTICE

For many years I instructed beginning ice courses, introducing hundreds of climbers to ice. In those years I developed a sense of how to get new climbers "flowing" on the ice. The key to rapid improvement is no mystery: put in mileage on the ice (on toprope) to gain confidence, good footwork, and efficient movement; and watch good climbers to see how they move, and to realize that basic ice climbs are not that hard.

Before leaving the ground on your first climb, practice swinging the tools into a variety of features—bulges, grooves, flat faces, etc. Experiment with your swing until you get a nice, snappy swing that sends the pick cleanly into the ice. When you finally leave the ground (on toprope), you must be solid on your feet to climb well. Plant your crampons with pizazz, and trust them—unlike rock climbing, you can make your footholds as good as you want. Never move a tool until both feet are well planted. Practice by toproping ice at a variety of angles. First climb with two tools, then one, then none (some guides encourage the opposite progression—no tools, then one, then two). It's amazing what you can climb without tools, laybacking and underclinging icicles, hand jamming ice slots, using old pick holes as monodoigts (thin gloves help here). Duncan Ferguson once led Vail's *Rigid Designator*, a vertical 120-foot ice fall without ice axes. Climbing without tools develops good crampon work, balance, weighting of the feet, and posture. And when you climb again with tools, you'll be more confident and efficient on your feet.

Another helpful exercise is to plant the axe or axes as few times as possible, making big moves on each placement. This helps break the energy-wasting error of making small moves. Practice downclimbing too, because when you start leading, the best way out of trouble is often to climb back down. Finally, explore the limits of your ice picks. See how little ice will hold you, and learn to avoid over-driving the picks (on toprope, of course).

Toprope practice allows you to safely explore your boundaries. You can try new techniques, and crank a lot of ice, with little risk.

*(opposite page)*
*The Fang, Vail, Colorado.*

Temperature, air bubbles, flowing water and direct sunshine dictate the hardness of ice. Conditions follow a continuum from bulletproof to brittle to plastic to slushy—sometimes in the same day. Brittle ice occurs when temperatures are well below freezing, and it tends to fracture in plates (called dinner plates) when you plant your tools. Brittle ice demands extra strength, patience, finesse, and ability to read the ice. Sometimes light swings, where you essentially tap the picks in, help prevent dinner plating. Other times, heavy blows clear the inevitable plates with the least effort. At temperatures near freezing and slightly above, ice becomes plastic. Picks sink into plastic ice like darts in a dart board; the climbing is fast, easy, and fun. As the temperature warms above freezing, ice gets soft and slushy. At its worst, slush ice will not support picks, front points, or ice screws—imagine trying to climb a vertical Slurpee. The opposite of slushy, soft ice is bulletproof ice—ice so cold and hard, and sometimes packed with dirt, gravel, or minerals, that picks have

## Beta for Beginners

*by* Joe Josephson

Are you psyched to finally try ice climbing? Good! But for God's sake, don't go out in January when it's so cold your toes and nose boogers freeze. If you do this, you'll never return for a second attempt. Find a time when it is relatively warm and the ice is good (not cold and brittle, or dripping wet). You'll learn to appreciate the masochism of bad ice soon enough.

In ice climbing, the main point of style is control. Far too often, ice climbs are completed at the expense of safety. Tools popping out of the ice, needlessly bombarding your belayer with ice, placing poor protection or shaking your way up a climb are all examples of poor style.

What about the style of using tethers to attach your tool(s) to your harness? One intermediate climber became so pumped on the crux pitch of the Canadian classic *Murchison Falls* WI4+ that he couldn't set pro or clip his tools. After watching his hands grease out of his mitts, he was rewarded with a broken ankle. In short, forget the ethics police who say tethers are uncool. Falling on ice climbs is downright dangerous. Tethers can improve your security when you're pushing your limits, but if you do hang from them, your tools better be well placed. Most advanced climbers forgo tethers, however—they rely on skill and experience to make up for the lack of tethers.

One of the biggest hazards in ice climbing is other climbers. Other climbers will knock off ice and invariably be slower than you (they're saying the same thing about you). Don't let others rush you or climb above or too close to you, no matter who they are. Stand your ground; no one has the right to endanger you.

Guidebooks help you learn what to expect, and give the grade of a route. Avoid getting caught up in the numbers game, though. Understand your abilities and limitations, and remember, on most routes the crux is finding and placing adequate protection.

a hard time penetrating. This brand of ice requires a brutish swing, and it's abusive to your picks.

Other factors also influence or indicate the condition of the ice. What color is the ice? Solid ice tends to be blue or blue-green. Sometimes it's stained yellow by minerals in the flow. White ice is aerated—often easy to climb, but difficult to protect well, unless you can find some blue ice underneath. How thick is the ice? Thin ice is harder to climb and protect than thick ice. How well is the ice bonded to the underlying rock? Ice formations frozen solid to the rock are strong and stable, but water flowing between the rock and ice undermines the ice strength. Unbonded thin ice is like a time bomb waiting to explode. Chandelier ice, composed of hundreds of small, partially fused icicles, is hard to climb and protect, because no solid core of ice exists. The new ice parks, such as in Ouray and Lee Vining, often have unstable, poorly bonded ice. Use care when choosing a line in these areas. Joe Josephson elaborates:

> Literally hundreds of ice types and formations exist. Over the years you'll encounter many of these—sometimes there will be half a dozen or more on a single pitch. To me, a truly good ice climber is a person that can deal with any ice form encountered. The ability to recognize, find protection in, and climb with grace and panache on any type of ice is perhaps the ultimate goal when learning to ice climb.
>
> Just about anyone, given enough strength and stupidity, can bash their way up hard ice climbs. But to climb effortlessly (or appear as such) and safely by using the features inherent in the formations and in the ice—by taking advantage of technology, by thinking about every placement and plotting every move ahead, and by using your body to move around and ultimately up the ice—is a much more difficult and dynamic skill.
>
> These skills may take longer to learn than straight-forward bashing, but you will be rewarded with a graceful and dynamic style that will keep the beauty of ice climbing alive for as long as you partake. Learn to climb in this way and you will never say ice climbing is boring.

## PLANNING THE LINE

Before starting up a route, study the features and pick your line. Look for good ice, and the path of least resistance. Often, even a vertical icefall offers an easier line of grooves and ramps. Features that allow stemming, like grooves and gullies, keep weight off your arms. Try to find a "hazard-free" line, with no hanging icicles or unstable ice above, and in the mountains, steer clear of lines below avalanche slopes, seracs and cornices. Look for stances for placing protection, or areas where you might get rock pro. If the climb is dripping or pouring water, avoid the drip line, or keep one tool in the drip line for easy sticks, but keep your body out so you stay dry. **On multi-pitch routes, always plan the line so the leader doesn't pummel the belayer with ice.**

An aggressive kick is the key to getting your crampon placed securely in cold ice. Eye the spot where you want to kick, then raise the foot so the lower leg is cocked about 90 degrees at the knee.

Let 'er rip. Kick forward like you're place-kicking a football.

One or two kicks will usually do it; over kicking wastes time and energy. Look, listen and feel to ensure a solid placement.

## The Kick

*by* Kim Csizmazia

Just kick it. Come on, wail it, bust out a foothold! Let the weight of your boot and crampon help swing your foot with purpose. Focused, energetic kicks are the goal, but make sure you pay attention to the nature of what you're kicking. If the ice is solid and thick just kick it like a football. On chandeliered ice, pay attention that your front points don't slip between or around icicles. Try to stab the icicles with your front points, or break them enough to clear the way to a good foot placement. For thin ice, make sharp little taps until you see your points grab, then stand up, keep your heels low, and trust it. Do not purposefully kick fragile ice that you want to use for upward progress. Instead, like a sensitive artist, tap delicate etchings and carvings.

One trick is to lightly tap edges and holes onto the icicle with your tools before starting up. Then when you are higher you can stand on these placements without having to kick the ice. Remember that you don't always have to kick. Place your feet on natural features whenever possible. One of my favorite moves is to high step onto a cauliflower or ice ledge and rock onto it so that I am sitting on my heel. Stay creative to keep up with the ever-changing ice medium.

Dual front points provide good stability. Keep the heels low to relax your calves and to engage both the front points and second row of points.

The heels are too high here, so the calves are stressed, the placement is wobbly, and the points are likely to shear through the ice.

Once you're climbing, you still have micro route finding decisions: namely, where to plant your tools and feet to conserve energy and move with style. These are covered below.

## THE FOUNDATION: FOOTWORK

As in rock climbing, good footwork yields efficient, fun movement, while poor footwork makes climbing sketchy, strenuous, and dangerous. Strive for flawless footwork.

Front pointing technique dominates on steep water ice. To set the front points, scan the terrain and pick the best place to step. The tops of low angle blobs and old pick holes make good footholds (mono-points were practically made for old pick holes); if none are available, choose a patch of smooth ice. Kick that spot until you have a secure crampon placement—one or two kicks should do unless the ice is brittle. Sharp crampons penetrate and hold much better than dull ones. Excessive kicking doesn't

Many climbers prefer mono-points for mixed climbs and difficult ice routes. Make sure the second row of points engages to give you a tripod of stability.

These mono-points are not placed deep enough, and the heels are too high, so this is an unstable stance.

Heels low and knees slightly bent relaxes your calves and your mind.

The classic rest step for water ice; one foot flat on a low angle patch of ice, and the other front pointing. Most of the weight is on the flat foot, with the leg straight to relax the quadriceps, and the ankle flexed so you get both rows of bottom points in the ice. If you can't get enough ankle flex (especially when wearing plastic boots), point the toes slightly downhill and flex at the Achilles tendon.

increase security, it only wastes time and energy, and destroys thin ice. When kicking, think about swinging your foot with enough force to penetrate the ice. As a follow-through, press firmly into the ice at the end of the kick so the points don't rebound.

Keep your feet about shoulder-width apart, unless you're stemming or using the ice features otherwise. Usually a series of short steps is easier than a high step, but high steps can work miracles, especially when pulling over a bulge.

Once planted, the crampons should be horizontal (unless you're stemming) and weighted with the calf relaxed. This position allows the second row of points to bite and fortify the front points. Hold your feet steady lest they sketch off the ice. Hinge body motion through your ankles to prevent excessive foot movement, and think consciously about keeping your heels low.

On all angles of ice up to vertical, your center of gravity should be directly over your crampon points. Vertical and steeper ice forces you to lean back, increasing the weight on your arms. On moderate ice you might stagger your crampon

Even on a tiny horizontal ledge, you can rest-step on the heel points to give your calves a break. Note the front points are hanging off the ice. When placing protection, you can sometimes save energy by chopping a small stance like this for a rest step.

On this small, sloping ledge you can cop a rest step by standing on the heel and pointing the toes downhill.

placements, setting one foot higher than the other. In this case, keep the lower leg straight, since it supports most of your weight. If you're resting, placing a screw, or climbing steep ice, set both crampons at the same level and distribute your weight between your legs. Keep your legs almost straight, with knees slightly bent, to relax your quadriceps.

French technique (flat footing) works great for resting, placing gear, or climbing low-angle ice. The key is to find a small platform and stomp firmly down onto it, rolling your ankle so both the inside and outside rails of points contact the ice. On steeper footholds, point your toes slightly downhill to keep both rails on the ice. If the hold is too small for the entire crampon, stand on the heel points. On water ice you'll usually flat foot only one foot at a time. That leg should bear most of your weight, so keep it straight with your center of gravity directly over the resting heel.

On low-angle ice you can reduce calf strain by front pointing one foot and flat footing the other (at three o'clock and nine o'clock); front pointing both feet is faster, though, so flat-foot technique is usually reserved for resting, standing on ledges, climbing low-angle water ice, and climbing alpine ice.

On a really basic level, four ice shapes dictate how you will use your feet. The easiest to climb is a groove or corner where you splay your feet outwards to stem and get the weight off your arms. More pumpy is a flat sheet of ice or large pillar, where you point the crampons straight in. A free-standing pencil or icicle forces you to climb pigeon-toed, which is very pumpy (although some tricks exist that are covered in Chapter 5). Finally, you have overhanging ice and ice roofs, which are also very pumpy, but you can reduce the weight on your arms by using back steps, drop knees, heel hooks, and stems.

Where to swing? If possible, find an old pick hole, or a spot that's slightly concave. A small patch of snow on the ice often indicates a weakness where the pick will plant easily. Also, use your reach to minimize the number of placements.

## GIVE IT THE AXE

### Planting Your Tools

*Where to strike?* Plant the tools high, without overextending, to minimize the number of placements required. The exception is if you have a close, easy placement. Experience enables you to read ice and know where to strike for the least effort. Thoughtfully choose each placement—depressions, concavities, divots, old pick holes, slightly wet spots, soft patches, and flat spots between icicles make good choices. Snow often accumulates in old pick holes, marking them like chalk on a rock route. Don't be afraid to cross your tools to take advantage of the "natural" holds. Go for the good, efficient placements, and move the rest of your body accordingly—this is the fun way to climb.

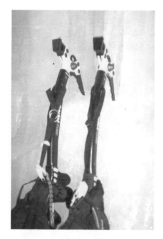

These tools are definitely too close together. Unless you're hooking into existing holes, planting the tools so close together risks fracturing a plate of ice, sending your axes and you flying. If the ice is soft, the picks should be planted at least 18 inches apart. In brittle ice, set them 2 feet or more apart.

## Planting Your Tools

Choose the spot where you want to swing and set your pick on it. This step is optional, but often helpful.

Wind up by bringing the tool back . . .

. . . a few inches above your shoulder, with your elbow bent around 90 degrees.

Swing the tool aggressively forward, while eyeing the spot you want to hit.

Near the end of the swing, snap your wrist forward. Much of the power of the swing comes from this wrist flick. Ideally, you want the pick to follow its axis into the ice; the more the pick of your axe droops downward, the more you want to flick the wrist to give the pick a downward trajectory.

As the pick enters, it displaces ice. Look to make sure the ice around the placement doesn't fracture, listen for a nice solid "Thunk!" and feel for a stout placement rather than a tinny, wobbly, vibrating one. If the placement isn't good, swing again at the exact same point.

A successful swing, with the pick well-placed but not over-buried.

## The Wrist Swing

1. In tight places or on thin ice, swing mostly from the wrist. Line up the pick on the point you want to strike (optional).

2. Wind up for the swing by flexing your wrist back. The elbow bends only slightly, with the axe lining up 60 to 90 degrees from the surface of the ice.

3. Snap the wrist forward and let the axe fly aggressively and precisely to the point you've selected.

4. As the pick enters the ice, look, listen, and feel to ensure that you have a secure placement. Swing again if you don't. In brittle ice, these tools might be too close together. A large dinner plate might take both tools out.

Avoid planting tools in convex sections of ice, such as bulges—they usually shatter. Don't set the tools close together, or you can fracture a plate that releases both axes, sending you flying. In bitter cold, thermal expansion and contraction creates ultra-thin cracks in the ice. Planting the pick dead center in a vertical crack, or a couple inches above a horizontal crack minimizes shattering. Good climbers don't usually knock much ice down, because they know where and how hard to swing. Careful attention to placement reduces plating in brittle ice.

To plant the tool, hold your axe just above the spike, and keep your wrist leashes adjusted perfectly to this length. Once you've carefully selected the choice spot, eye that point like a bull's-eye and strike it until you have a good plant. A solid placement may take a single swing if the ice is plastic, or if a hole exists. Or it may take several swings in brittle ice. Sometimes, you'll first reach the pick to the point you want to hit. This is especially helpful when "feeling" around for holes. Now wind the tool up by raising and bending your elbow, then whip the tool forward. At the last instant, snap your wrist to pop the axe forward, letting momentum carry the pick home. The wrist snap is crucial: it imparts a sharp downward thrust to the swing, so the pick strikes the ice along its axis, minimizing shattering and maximizing penetration. Like a good carpenter drives nails, you're not pushing the axe into the ice; rather, you're giving the tool momentum so it can drive itself in.

*If there's a lot of snow on the ice, use the axe to brush it clear before planting your pick so you can see where you're striking.*

Look, listen and feel as the pick hits the ice. *Look* to be sure cracks don't shoot out from the placement. *Listen* for a solid "THUNK!" rather than a tinny shattering or shearing sound. *Feel* for the pick to drive home. When the plant is solid, you can feel the vibrations dampen from the pick to the shaft. Set the pick an inch or two into *good* ice. Don't move on sketchy placements, but also don't overbury the tool—unlike Lizzie Borden, it doesn't take 40 whacks to set your axe. Once you get a good plant, trust it and go. Trusting the tools is spooky at first, especially on steep ice, but hesitation makes climbing harder. Tool testing (described on the next page) makes it easier to relax and trust your placements.

Styles for swinging axes run the spectrum, from the burly Neanderthal slam to a precise surgeon's peck. Most good climbers swing somewhere in between, favoring a subtle but snappy swing in most conditions, and getting burly when conditions dictate, such as in cold, brittle ice. When the ice is riddled with old pick holes or natural pockets, go with a soft touch. Hook your picks in the holes, or set them lightly, clawing catlike over the ice. If holes don't exist, a good swing sets the pick.

Some climbers favor a subtle windup, powering the swing through the wrist snap. This works well with steeply drooped picks, because it imparts the necessary downward thrust. With a radically drooped pick you can also pull your elbow down *slightly* to finish the swing, which gives downward thrust and sets the teeth. This *elbow drop* works wonders for beginners who are having difficulty executing a good wrist snap.

Other climbers prefer a hefty windup, with a wrist snap at the end. A strong windup gives more forward velocity to the pick. A brawny power throw works when the ice is cold and thick, but trashes your picks in thin ice—you'll dull the picks, and maybe break them. If you whack too hard in plastic ice, you'll get the pick stuck and have a tiring battle removing it. Instead, plant your picks with an eye for removing them.

*How deep should you bury the pick? It depends on the quality of the ice, whether or not you're hooking an existing pick hole, the style of pick you're using, and whether you're toproping, leading, or soloing. If you're leading, your distance above good protection will come into play also. The more jeopardy you're in, the more important it is to have solid plants. This pick is probably deeper than it needs to be, unless the ice is very soft. Buried this deep, it might be difficult to remove.*

Different shaft and pick shapes require different swings. If you switch tools, modify your swing so the pick strikes the ice in the direction of its axis.

If the ice is brittle or rotten, use your pick to clear the bad surface layer before planting your tool—usually you can find good ice beneath the surface. Sometimes two sharp blows a few inches apart, both angled toward the center of a dinner plate, will clear the surface layer. Experiment—different conditions require different techniques. If the ice isn't brittle, just plant the tool; only clear the surface layer if you fracture a dinner plate or to place an ice screw. Two hard judgement calls are knowing if your blow started a dinner plate or not (it's usually but not always obvious), and on a subsequent blow, if your pick has reached solidly beneath the plate. Be conservative and reset the pick if in doubt. It's unnerving when a dinner plate knocks one of your crampons free. If your partner has been forced to belay directly below (something you should avoid), do whatever you can to avoid showering him or her with ice. Turn your face away from falling dinner plates, or duck your head and let your helmet do its job (bloody faces are common); and wear glasses or goggles (which often fog at the worst possible moment), or at least close your eyes when the pick hits the ice.

*A beat-out ice climb.*

After planting a pick, keep your hand pressed near the ice for stability. Avoid torquing on the shaft, as this can undermine the placement. With the newfound popularity of ice climbing, many routes become totally hacked up by midseason. Pockmarked ice can be easy to climb—you just hook your way up it.

*When the pick enters the ice, a lot of debris flies back. Either wear protective eyewear, duck your head, or . . .*

*. . . close your eyes at the moment of impact.*

### Knuckle Busters

One common beginner error, which even plagues experts occasionally, is smashing your knuckles against the ice. Knuckle bashing is painful, especially if you bash every swing. Bashing usually stems from too weak of a wrist snap. If you really pop the tool at the end of the swing, you'll keep your knuckle clear of the ice. Bashing also occurs if there's a protruding bulge in the ice that you didn't see. Bent grip and bent shaft tools help prevent bashing, and padded gloves can reduce the pain.

Occasionally, if a bulge protrudes where the shaft should rest, I'll clear the bulge before planting the tool. Bent shaft tools avoid this problem, because the bend clears such bulges.

### Removing Tools

To remove a tool, lever the shaft in and out so the top edge of the pick slices through the ice. If you get a tool stuck, work it a little harder, or ratchet the axe head up and down to work the pick out. Some climbers like to pop the adze or hammer head with the palm of their hand to free the tool. Never wrench the axe sideways—that's the best way to break the pick.

On toprope you can experiment to discover how a tiny speck of good ice will hold you—you'll be amazed! You'll also be dismayed by how easily picks shear through rotten ice. Practice to see how hard and deep to set the picks. Try different swinging techniques to see what works best, and when. Stay open-minded when learning, and keep your face away from a loaded tool, lest you eat the hammer or adze if the tool pops.

When climbing in balance over your feet, you can go with less secure pick placements because the picks hold little weight. On steep ice, where the picks do hold a lot of weight, plant them securely, especially if you're leading. Sometimes you can set one pick less than bomber, provided you reset it first on the next move.

### Hook and Stack

The best way to save energy when planting your tools is to hook them in old pick holes (when seconding or on recently climbed routes), or in natural holes, pockets, or crevices between icicles. If the hole is relatively deep and supported by good ice, a hook placement is bomber—especially with re-curved or drooped picks. Generally, you want to move the tools as far as possible between placements (without overreaching), but if good hooking holds appear, shorten the moves (or lengthen them) to utilize the hooking placements. If I'm leading or soloing, I'll often set the hook placement with a very light swing. This way the teeth bite for security, and I can feel the ice to make sure it's sturdy, which helps calm my mind.

You can also save time and energy by stacking tools—hooking one pick over the other. This is more of an advanced technique, used when the good ice is patchy and you can't find placements wherever you want them. It's also useful when pulling the lip of an

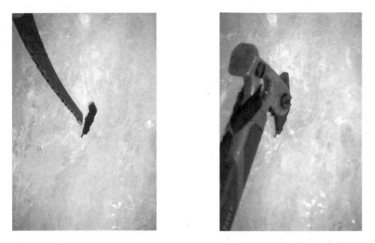

When hooking an existing hole, you can often just set the pick in the hole.

If the hooking hole isn't very deep, or if you want some extra security, it's good to give the pick a slight outward yank at the end of a light swing to set the pick. This keeps the pick from wobbling around in the hole, and lets you test the strength of the ice.

overhang, moving onto a hanging ice curtain, and for minimizing ice disturbance when climbing a fragile ice structure. Make sure the planted pick is good, because the whole shooting match rides on it.

## Testing the Placement

In questionable ice, test your placements before moving on them, to increase your safety and confidence. This is similar to testing placements in hard aid climbing. The more dangerous a potential fall is, the more important it becomes to the test. Test a placement by rolling your shoulder down, putting gentle body weight in the direction of pull (straight down along the axis of the shaft). Make sure the first tool placement is good before testing the second one, to avoid ripping both tools out. Don't wriggle the pick up and down, which can subvert the placement, and don't "bounce" on the tool; this only wastes energy. Once you've tested the tool, relax and crank the move—no need to hesitate, because you know the placement is solid.

Testing wastes energy in good, thick ice. Instead, judge placements by how they look, sound, and feel.

A T-stack works when there's only enough ice for one pick, and also to save energy when pulling an ice roof. Make sure the set pick is well placed!

*If you're not sure about the placement, you can test it by rolling your shoulder down and weighting the tool straight-armed. Testing placements is a good technique in bad ice, or when climbing far above good protection, but overuse of tool testing wastes energy. In good ice, it's better to learn how to judge a solid placement by the way it feels and sounds.*

Still, if I'm soloing, or leading way above protection, I may test my placements to help cool my mind, even if the ice is bomber.

## THE FLOW

*You may have heard of the X-body position, but this isn't it. This climber's so stiff, he appears to be crucified on the ice.*

The road to fluidity on ice is a long one. Each time you climb, focus on one or two technique refinements—you can't improve everything at once. With practice your body will move automatically, exactly the way you trained it. For this reason, it's important to learn good technique, so you don't get stuck with bad habits. The ice climbing ace moves with obvious ease because his body runs on autopilot, with little thought required—until the going gets hard, that is.

Use techniques appropriate for the angle of ice you're on. As the angle changes, make smooth transitions between techniques, like a crack climber switches techniques for different size cracks.

Similar to old school rock climbing, keep three points of contact on the ice at all times—no dynos here. Move one tool or crampon at a time, and work each placement until it's good. Moving on sketchy placements is scary and dangerous—and it's one of the most common beginner errors. The key lies in absolute control!

*Stay loose, and take the holds that present themselves, as if you're climbing rock. With this attitude, you'll often find yourself in non-linear positions, moving efficiently. Keep your arms straight whenever possible to minimize the load on your biceps.*

## Think Rock

Many rock climbing techniques and body positions work well on ice. If you're proficient on rock, you've got a good start. Now, learn the nuances and intricacies of ice, and apply your established rock climbing techniques. First, avoid being stiff on ice. Instead, strive for fluid, confident, relaxed movement. Some rock techniques that work great on ice are shown in the accompanying photos.

*Climbing with arms straight is important on rock as well as ice.*

When you do lock off, bring your shoulder close to your hand to minimize the leverage on your biceps.

Stemming is one of the best techniques for saving energy on steep ice and steep rock.

The twist lock, where you lock off with your arm tight across your chest and turn your hip into the ice minimizes the load on your arms and extends your reach on steep ice as well as rock. On ice, the hip turn is often subtle.

A hip scum, where you rest your hip against a corner of rock or ice, can be a very restful position.

Heel hooking allows you to use your leg as a third hand. On ice it's more often used to maintain balance, while on rock the heel hook often supports a lot of body weight.

Laybacking isn't that common on ice, but in mixed climbing you do what's necessary to make the holds work. Vertically oriented holds often work best when laybacked.

## LOW ANGLE (40 TO 60 DEGREES)

Try cruising low-angle ice with only one tool. If you're leading, though, two tools add security. It's a drag leaning over to set your picks on low-angle ice. You can hold the pick like a cane, and stick the spike in the ice for balance, especially on soft ice. For more security, plant the pick and make long moves, mantling over your axe before resetting it. To mantle your axe, plant it high and walk your feet up. Move your hand to the axe head and move your feet higher, until the axe is below your waist, with your arm straight above it. Now reset the axe and repeat. Front point with both feet, or flat foot one and front point the other. If you front point, throw in the occasional flat foot for resting.

This angle is easy to follow or toprope with only one tool, and mantling the tool allows you to minimize the number of plants. If you're using two tools, stagger the placements: set one tool high, move the feet up two or three steps, then set the other tool high. Move the feet again before resetting the first tool. Staggering the placements cuts the number of placements in half, saving time and energy.

On super low-angle water ice, you can flat foot with both feet, set one pick in the ice for security, and plant the other tool's spike for balance.

Another technique for low-angle ice is to climb with just one tool to minimize the number of pick placements. A combination of flat footing and front pointing works well here. When you're balanced with the flat foot lower than the front point foot, set the pick high. See the following sequence for more detail.

*Low angle ice technique: Walk your feet up, . . .*

*. . . then put your hand on the head of the axe and mantle it.*

*If you're very secure on your feet, or if you have a toprope, remove the pick and reset it high.*

*If you're feeling insecure, or if you're leading and want an axe always placed for safety, leave the tool planted at waist level and set the second tool high.*

*Then step your feet up as high as possible . . .*

*. . . and reset the first axe.*

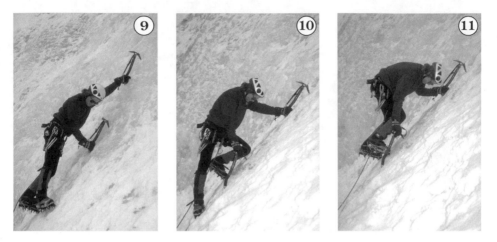

*Once you've set the axe securely, walk your feet up, then move your hand to the head of the axe to mantle it, and walk your feet up again, as high as you can. Now it's time to reset the second axe and start over.*

### MODERATE (60 TO 75 DEGREES)

*Glen Murray enjoying moderate ice in Boulder Canyon, Colorado.*

Routes of this angle are pretty straightforward: front point with both feet and stagger tool placements. Feet can be at the same level to share your weight, staggered for speed, or stemmed for efficiency. On all angles below vertical, keep your center of gravity over your feet. Flat foot when you see a nice platform to stand on.

While you want to plant your picks high to minimize the number of placements, avoid overreaching, which forces you to raise your heels.

### GETTIN' STEEP (75 TO 85 DEGREES)

This is where ice begins to feel vertical, because it's in your face. Axe moves get shorter, but still, spread the placements far to minimize the number of tool plants. Strong climbers can stagger their placements for speed and efficiency. Intermediate and beginning climbers might move both tools up, then both feet, then repeat, especially as the ice approaches verticality. Stem or use other rock climbing positions when possible to lighten the load on your arms.

### VERTICAL (85 TO 95 DEGREES)

Vertical ice often feels overhanging—especially during your first forays onto steep ice. Because your arms support a lot of weight, keep them straight whenever possible. When you must lock off, keep your hand tight to your shoulder to conserve bicep strength.

Also, hang from tightened wrist leashes, rather than a death grip on your tools, to spare your forearms. Strive for precise, efficient tool placements—don't thrash, or move the tools only a few inches at a time. Borrow from the vast arsenal of rock climbing techniques wherever possible, stemming, twist-locking, and back stepping your way to efficiency and fun. Mixing up techniques to alternate the muscle groups that get stressed is key to avoiding getting pumped. Most important, keep your mind and body relaxed.

Again, plant your tools high, without overextending. On this angle, overextending raises your heels, and it can put an outward pull on the planted tool which may pop it out (bad surprise!). Also, if you try to plant the tool too high and you get a poor stick, it's hard to remove it to get a good stick.

## ICE TECHNIQUE

### The Monkeyhang

The pure monkeyhang technique is retrograde, because it's stiff and regimented. Nonetheless, the concepts of the monkeyhang—straight arms, tight lock offs, and resting on vertical ice—are crucial. The monkeyhang is easy to learn, so it offers a platform from which to add more sophisticated moves.

*Once the ice turns vertical or slightly beyond, the principles of the monkeyhang work well, though the technique is a bit rigid. The basis of the monkeyhang is to keep your arms as straight as possible. With both tools planted high, and both arms straight and relaxed, bring both feet up while keeping your arms straight. In the pure monkeyhang, your feet are often level with each other. From this position, you might loosen the pick that you intend to reset first so it comes out easily when you're locked off. Then stand up and lock off with your shoulder tight to your hand. (Sequence continued next page.)*

*4. Remove the tool you've previously loosened, and reset it high.*

*5. As soon as you have a good placement, transfer your weight to the high, straight-armed tool.*

*6. Now reset the lower tool, . . .*

*7. . . . and repeat the monkeyhang sequence.*

The monkeyhang goes like this:
- Plant a tool high and immediately hang straight-armed from the wrist leash.
- Set the second tool 2 feet or so sideways from the first tool, to avoid blowing out both placements, then distribute your weight between both straight arms.
- Bring both feet up, with your knees bent and your butt out. Now you can rest for the next move, with your weight suspended on straight arms and tight wrist leashes. You might loosen the tool you intend to replant first, for quick removal in the next step. If one tool is planted less bomber than the other, move it up first.
- Pull up and lock off with your shoulder tight to the tool to minimize the leverage on your biceps. Reset the other tool high and immediately transfer weight from the locked-off arm to the new placement, with your arm straight. Repeat steps two through four until you come to the gruesome bulge topping the pillar . . .

The monkeyhang works for climbing steep, unfeatured ice. Whenever possible, add stems, backsteps, and twist-locks to the monkeyhang, and stagger your tool placements. Usually, these rock climbing techniques allow more grace and ease than the monkeyhang, which is rigid and requires brutish lock-off strength.

## Back stepping

Back stepping may be a slight misnomer on ice. On rock, back stepping means standing on the outside edge of your foot and twisting your hip in, to extend your reach and lighten the load on your arms. On ice, you rarely stand on the outside edges of your feet, but you can twist your hip in. Isolated moves or a sequence of back stepping saves energy on steep ice. When back stepping, you can move your feet, then both tools, then your feet; but it's often more efficient, if you have good enough technique, to stagger the tool placements, even on steep ice. The back stepping sequence goes like this:

(1) Plant both picks, step up and back step the left foot if you have a ledge or bump to stand on. If not, front point with the left toes angling slightly right. Turn the left hip into the ice, and "flag" the right foot.

(2) Twist-lock off the right tool by drawing your right hand into your chest, and twisting your left shoulder in and up. Now plant the left tool high and hang straight-armed from it.

(3a) Reset the left foot so you face straight into the ice and plant the right tool high; or

(3b) bring both feet up, reverse your hips and back step right. Then plant the right tool high and carry on. This second option involves staggering your tool placements, which demands clever use of the ice features, but requires fewer tool plants.

Back stepping decreases the required lock-off strength, and increases your reach by a couple of inches, but requires foot and

*1. Back stepping works well on steep ice, though the actual back step is more subtle than in rock climbing. Rather than actually standing on the outside edge of your boot (like in rock climbing), you're often kicking the crampon in at an angle, and twisting your hip in to extend your reach and minimize the weight on your locked-off arm. Do this by twisting your left hip in when setting the left tool high, and . . .*

*2. . . . twisting your right hip in when setting the right tool.*

*3. The twist lock maximizes your reach and minimizes the effort. Roll your body and turn your hip in so the locked off arm folds across the chest. Now plant the next tool high.*

hip savvy, and the right ice features. Many variations exist—the key is to fluidly and creatively combine techniques.

## *Stemming*

Ice falls are rarely smooth and featureless. Usually you can find features to stem on, such as grooves, icicles, ice bumps, or rock

Stemming a shallow groove.

*If the ice features allow, you can get a more pronounced backstep going.*

*1. Stemming is one of the most valuable energy-saving techniques in ice climbing. Here the climber is stemming between two pillars, which makes steep ice far less strenuous. Note he's also crossing his tools, setting up for a move to the right (or going for a better placement than he could get above and left of his right tool).*

*2. Here the climber is stemming between two ice pillars and twisting his hip into the ice to extend his reach.*

Stemming across a groove or concave face of ice can make light work out of vertical ice.

*Even a very shallow stem between two minor ice features saves energy.*

edges, to relieve your arms. Even a shallow stem between two ice bumps can be beneficial. On steep ice, the value of stemming cannot be overstated.

## High Step

Most of the time, several short steps require less energy than leg-pumping high steps. High steps come into their own for moving between widely spaced footholds, bypassing stretches of bad ice, or making the final move over an ice bulge.

Generally, you want to make short steps up the ice, but when passing a bulge, even a minor one as shown, it often helps to high step.

High stepping also works well for moving between good footholds.

The frog move comes in handy sometimes when you want to bring your feet up high to use a good foothold, and still keep your body in close to the ice.

## Reaching-through and Stepping-through

Normally your body will have some type of X position. But when the features dictate, or when traversing, it's often helpful to reach-through, crossing one tool over the other, or one foot in front of the other. It's also helpful to cross the tools whenever it allows you to get easier placements. The next move will be to uncross.

Be creative with the X-body posture. You can cross your tools to set up for a move sideways, or to go for an easy hook move rather than creating your own pick hole.

The same goes for crossing your legs—you can cross legs to set up for a step-through or to best utilize the available footholds.

## Staggering

Even on steep ice, good climbers often stagger their tool placements, except when they're really pumped. Even though you have to lock off a little harder, staggering tools requires fewer placements, for an overall increase in efficiency—if you're strong. Staggering also gives you more options for where to plant each tool; if you're planting one tool 2 feet above the other, you can set it anywhere in that horizontal space, *without* getting too close to the other tool. With both tools on the same level, you have to work harder to keep them far enough apart. Because the placements are spread farther when you stagger, you have less chance of plating both tools out of the ice, so it's safer.

To stagger, move the first tool, then both feet, move the second tool, and again move both feet, ad nauseam. If you need a rest on steep terrain, it's better to plant the tools side by side (not too close!), and hang straight-armed from both axes.

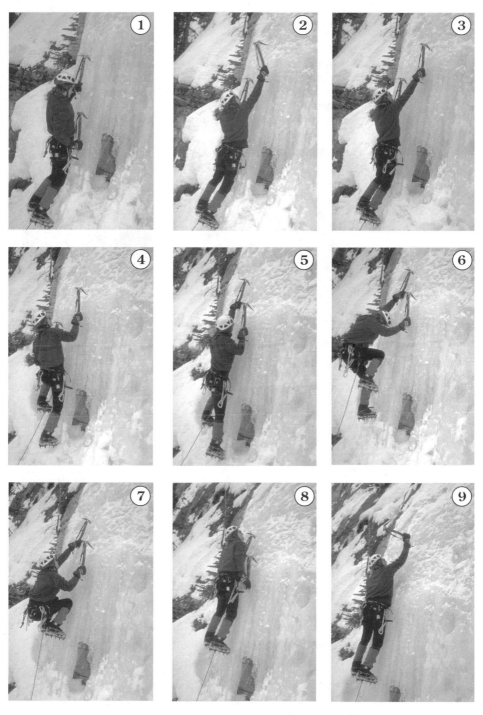

You can save a lot of energy by staggering your placements and setting the picks half as often. With the left tool high and the right tool low, reset the right tool. Once it's securely planted, walk both feet up, and reset the left tool. Take at least two steps up, stand up, and reset the right tool. Stagger your pick placements whenever you can.

## Free Hand

Don't feel constrained in your ice tools. If natural handholds present themselves, holster the tool, or let it hang from your wrist, and grab that icicle or cauliflower, jam that space between icicles, mantle that ice bump. You can save time and energy by not planting your tools, but you give up some security, so make sure your feet are well planted.

Who says you have to have both axes planted all the time? Sometimes you can save time and energy by using your hands rather than your axes on ice features. Often, though, when leading, I prefer to hook my pick if possible for improved security.

Another natural handhold. This one will also make a great foothold when the climber gets higher.

## RESTING

On steep terrain, seeking and using rests will keep your guns firing. Rests come in many forms—a small ice ledge, a hip scum against a pillar, a stem, a drop knee in a small ice cave, a leg draped over an ice hump, a chimney position between the ice and rock. You can even chop a small foot ledge with your axe. On marginal rests, you can alternately switch the hands or feet supporting you, to offer each stressed muscle group some rest. While resting, relax your mind and muscles, to recover for the upcoming moves. On lead, set protection from rest positions whenever possible. Good resting technique can be crucial for success on an enduro pitch.

On steep ice, a hip scum against a pillar is a great way to rest your guns.

Stemming is a good way to cop a rest on steep terrain.

Here, a drop knee and a flat foot provide a great rest on the outside of a small ice cave.

Ride 'em cowboy! Sometimes you can drape your leg over an ice bump or through a hole to get a good rest.

The hanging pillar to the right of the climber provides rest for several moves. First the climber is using a shoulder scum to relieve some weight from the arms.

As he moves up, a hip scum opposed by a left-foot stem supports a lot of body weight.

Finally, his thigh jammed against the pillar and opposed by the left foot keeps weight off his arms. Rest well here, because it's time to leave the rest after this move.

You can get a hands-off rest by chimneying between an ice pillar and the rock behind it, or between two ice pillars.

On steep ice without good resting features, you can still give your arms and hands a break by hanging straight-armed from your tools with the wrist leashes supporting your weight, and consciously relaxing your hands.

## PULLING THE DREADED BULGE

Many vertical or near vertical stretches of ice end in the dreaded bulge, where the ice recedes quickly to a lower angle. If you're lucky, the ice doesn't run out altogether, leaving you to scratch around on dirt, willow twigs, smooth rock or sugar snow. Pulling a bulge is often the crux, even with ample ice. When leading, consider setting protection just below the bulge. To clear a bulge, work your tools past the lip. Avoid setting them in the lip, or you'll dinner plate the ice. It's awkward swinging above the bulge, and difficult evaluating your placements because you can't see them. It helps to pull your elbow back (toward your body) at the end of the swing to plant a re-curved pick over a bulge. Keep your weight out so you can see your feet, and step up. Set your crampons well, because this is the last place you want to be sketching. Now advance the tools without leaning in or raising your heels. Step up again, high step over the lip, and stand up.

You can also plant a tool off to the side, and semi-layback over the top of the bulge. The main points are to set your tools and crampons well, keep your balance, and don't lean in too much. If you can't find ice over the bulge, good luck. Plant the tools in dirt you hope is frozen, dry tool on rock edges, plant the shaft in snow, or hook tree branches or roots; set your crampons well, and balance on your feet.

One final tip offered by Joe Josephson is to set the tools as high as possible in the vertical ice just below the bulge (not in the bulge, which will almost always dinner plate). Then high step, and reach far over the bulge with the tools.

The bulge at the top of a pillar is often the crux of a climb. By then you're often pumped, and you might be runout above your protection. It's difficult swinging your tools above the bulge and moving your body around it. But with good technique, the worst bulges can be overcome. When approaching a tricky bulge, try to have good protection within a reasonable distance (photo 1). Sometimes the top of a bulge is covered with snow. Use your axe to clear the snow so you can see where you're striking (photo 2 and 3). (Sequence continued next page.)

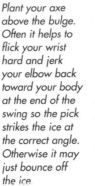

**4** Plant your axe above the bulge. Often it helps to flick your wrist hard and jerk your elbow back toward your body at the end of the swing so the pick strikes the ice at the correct angle. Otherwise it may just bounce off the ice.

**5** Now bring your feet up while leaning back so you can see where you're kicking.

**6** After setting your feet, stand up and set your second tool above the bulge. Place it close enough to the bulge so you can lean back and see your foot placements, but avoid setting it too close to the first tool.

**7** Work the feet up again, without leaning in too much.

**8** Then high step over the top of the bulge.

**9** You can then mantle your lower axe—or set it higher—and bring both feet past the bulge.

## PACING

Pacing means finding a good compromise between hasty, sloppy movement, and sluggish hesitation. Every climber has an optimal pace which allows him or her to keep the flow going and climb with calculated, efficient movement. Don't stall out, but do take time to find the choice footholds and tool placements, subtle rests, and the best line. Ice climbing in general is slow compared to rock climbing, but if you just keep moving you'll finish the pitch in reasonable time, and your partners will appreciate it.

## TRAVERSING

Sometimes you'll traverse to follow the path of least resistance, or to exit your belay ledge or cave to get back on the chosen line. Traversing is like climbing up, except you work your placements sideways. Often the leading tool's pick holes make nice holes for the trailing tool. Sometimes you'll step through with your feet, or reach through with your tools. You may angle the tools slightly, and move by pulling down and sideways on the tools. Because you're not moving up, you can keep your arms straight most of the time. Tubular picks work well on traverses, because you can rotate them in their placement. Be careful not to rotate blade picks as you traverse. Practice traversing by climbing across the bottom of a flow.

When traversing, you have many options for moving sideways. Here, the climber has placed the left tool directly above the right.

Now he widens his stance, and plants the right tool far to the right.

Shuffling his feet sideways, he sets up the next ice axe move.

Crossing over allows large sideways moves and fewer axe placements than shuffling the tools, but shuffling allows you to use old pick holes. After the cross over, uncross the tools.

You can also step-through when traversing. Pass your moving foot in front of the stationary foot and kick a good foot placement. Now uncross your legs to continue the traverse.

## DOWNCLIMBING

If you lead, you want to be proficient at downclimbing, so you have a bailout strategy that beats jumping off (not an option on ice because you risk fracturing an ankle if the crampon points snag the ice). Sometimes you'll downclimb easy ice to descend a route. Downclimbing is basically the reverse of climbing up, except your moves will be shorter. Plant your tools low, move the feet down until your arms are almost straight, and repeat. Using pick holes that you created on the way up helps. On steep ice, lean back to see the footholds, then regain proper posture and set the crampons where the holds are. This is especially important when climbing down a bulge. You can also set the axes down and off to the side, which makes it easier to get solid plants, and semi-layback the tools as you move down.

*Downclimbing low angle ice. Set the axe and take two or three steps down.*

*Reset the axe and continue.*

When downclimbing steep ice, it helps to lean back and see where you want to kick the foot.

Then lean back in and plant the foot solidly.

We've covered many tips for climbing efficiently in this chapter. To sum them up:

- Climb in a natural, flowing, rock climbing style.
- Stay relaxed.
- Keep your weight on your feet.
- Learn to plant your tools and crampons effectively.
- Use the fewest swings possible to get up the route (while still making good axe placements).
- Don't overdrive your tools.
- Stagger axe placements.
- Hook whenever the opportunity presents itself.
- When in doubt, test your placements so you can relax and move without fear.
- Learn to read the ice, so you know where to set the tools with the least effort.
- Keep the arms straight as much as possible.
- Hang from the wrist leashes, and don't overgrip.
- Use the proper technique for the angle of ice that you're on.
- Rest by standing flat-footed whenever you find natural stances.
- Turn your hips in (back step) on steep ice.
- Put mileage in on the ice, striving to climb as effortlessly and stylishly as possible.
- Stem, stem, stem.

A frequent beginner's error on steep ice is to climb with poor body position. Here, the climber's weight is too far out during the lockoff phase, so he's wasting a lot of strength in his left arm; he should be standing straight on his legs to plant his tool as high as possible.

On steep ice it's critical to hang from the wrist leash, rather than hold your tools with a death grip. This climber is going to get pumped—and fast.

Heels are way too high. This classic beginner's error makes a very unstable stance and pumps out your calves.

## Common Mistakes

- Climbing ice without a helmet
- Moving on sloppy tool/crampon placements
- Placing bad ice screws
- Leading or soloing with insufficient experience
- Belaying under a climber
- Planting the tools too close together
- Inefficient or ineffective testing of placements
- Heels too high
- Excessive kicking to set the crampons
- Resetting the tools too low
- Overextending to plant your tools
- Moving the feet in their placements
- Passing rest steps or using them inefficiently
- Setting tools, crampons, and/or ice screws in the wrong places
- Leaning in, especially on bulges
- Wrist leash not supporting weight
- Overgripping, being scared, tense, panicky, or hesitating
- Overplanting the tools
- Lifting the tools as you move past
- Pulling too hard with the arms
- Placing the tools too close together
- Feet too close together
- Front pointing steep ice with all the weight on one leg
- Keeping arms bent which strains the biceps
- Face behind the tool on steep ice (looking for a broken nose anyone?)
- Falling

Hang onto your tools!

The lobotomy move. Holding your face or forehead behind a loaded adze is a bad idea. If the pick blows, you could lose an eyeball, nose, lip, or a chunk of your brain.

# CHAPTER 5

# Advanced Technique

*"Fat ice is boring."*

The past 25 years have brought revolutionary equipment, techniques, and attitudes to ice climbing. Climbs once viewed as out of condition, either because they're too thin, too precarious, or altogether lacking ice, have become sought-after testpieces.

High-end routes often give a double whammy—harder moves and worse protection. Sometimes the formations are even threatening to fall down. These engaging routes not only require superior technique and strength, they also demand a cool head. Pushing the standards means drawing a fine line between boldness and stupidity. Many an ice maestro has taken a wild ride on a broken ice pillar. Most have been lucky not to be crushed to death by the tons of ice. Don't assume that you'll be so lucky.

Many contemporary routes follow a new direction—preplaced protection. With fixed gear, climbers can stretch their limits without the nagging threat of being maimed or killed if they make a mistake. This "sport" ice climbing requires exceptional fitness and technique, without demanding extreme boldness. Whichever direction you pursue, refined technique will help you climb ever-harder routes.

Why reinvent the wheel? Techniques already exist for climbing extreme vertical and overhanging terrain. Once again we stress rock climbing techniques, this time for climbing imperfect ice, thin smears, hanging pillars, and mixed routes.

## OVERHANGING ICE

Because gravity pulls water down toward the center of the earth, the steepest ice flows tend to be vertical. Yet sometimes, if the flow runs off an overhanging precipice of rock, strange forces create pillars or sheets of overhanging ice. You can also find radically steep ice on some glacial seracs. This is where pure ice climbing becomes brutally physical.

Rarely will you climb radically overhanging ice, unless you're pulling a roof or climbing a serac. Usually, a pillar leans no more than 5 or 10 degrees past vertical, so the techniques described above for water ice—the monkeyhang, back step, drop knee, and stemming—do the trick. You just have to crank harder on the tools, and work harder to place protection.

The starts to the third and fourth pitches of *French Reality* in the Canadian Rockies overhang. On the third pitch, small cauliflowers grant footholds so you can snake your body upward without getting massively pumped—until you fire in protection. On the fourth pitch, stemming between pillars offers a technical

*opposite page:*
*Dave Thomson working out the extended rock section of Stairway to Heaven (M7) on Mount Wilson, Alberta.*

JOE JOSEPHSON PHOTO

*Joe Josephson cranking yet another new route, this time in the Gaspé region of Quebec.* BERNARD MAILHOT PHOTO

solution to the overhanging ice. In thin conditions, the overhanging pillar of *Hot Doggies* in Colorado has no features for stemming or stepping on, so you have to hang on tight and pump it out.

The place you can find radically overhanging ice faces is on glacial seracs. Stevie Haston calls these monsters, "the future of pure ice climbing." The trouble is, seracs have a nasty habit of falling down. Pushed downwards with zillions of tons of pressure from the glacier above, seracs peel off without warning. Avoiding the heat of day really won't help you here.

Climbing icebergs presents an *exotic* deviation in ice climbing, for those flush with cash and free time to charter a ship to the far northern or deep southern seas, or for the upper echelon of sponsored climbers. Here, the main hazards include falling into the icy sea, having the iceberg capsize (or calve) and the actual boat ride in the arctic or antarctic seas.

A drop knee provides a perfect rest before exiting out onto this ice roof.

Laybacking off the tool and leaning on the icicle helps get the climber into position to pull this ice roof.

A backhand swing is often the ticket for exiting from rock out to an ice roof.

Stemming between the rock and icicle gets a lot of weight on your feet, even on overhanging terrain.

1. Executing a "Figure-Four" may help you pull ice roofs when no footholds exist.

2. Bring one leg up between your ice tools; be careful not to slice your parka.

3. Hook your knee over your elbow, flag your other leg off the roof, wrench your body up, . . .

4. . . . and plant the tool high.

## CAULIFLOWERS

Strange to look at, and even stranger to climb, cauliflowers form in the splash zone of some climbs, usually near the ground, or above a prominent ledge. Cauliflowers resemble the out-turned scales of a pine cone, and they vary in size from a couple of feet to several feet high. The size of the cauliflowers determines the technique you'll use to climb them.

Cauliflowers are often more solid than they appear—but not always. It's wise to test them before committing. On the crux of *French Reality*, two large cauliflowers broke when I barely touched them. This was unnerving because I was 25 feet above a ledge, climbing overhanging ice, with no possibility for good protection.

The *Rigid Designator* in Vail, Colorado always forms about 30 feet of 3-foot-high cauliflowers at the bottom. These are easy to climb—you grab them with your hands, or hook them with your

*Approaching giant cauliflowers at the base of Whiteman Falls, Alberta, Canada.*

When climbing cauliflowers, don't be afraid to let the tools dangle and climb free handed.

You can also hook your tools over the tops of the cauliflowers.

Let your body flow around the cauliflowers.

tools (more secure), and step from the top of one cauliflower to the next.

On *Repetence Super* in Val d'Aosta, Italy, the first pitch involved 100 feet of 7- to 8-foot-high cauliflowers. We'd do two overhanging moves to reach over one, then do a combination layback/mantle to surmount it, then regroup and do it over. After a dozen such boulder problems, we reached the belay. Protection was often a slung cauliflower.

*Whiteman Falls* in Alberta had towering cauliflowers at its base. We were there in late season, and the cauliflowers were so precarious I wouldn't get near them. Somehow we found a way to skirt around these nightmarish obstacles.

## CHANDELIER ICE

Chandelier ice—beautiful to look at, but often terrifying to climb. Chandelier ice consists of hundreds of tiny icicles, fused into a delicate matrix of ice and air. If no solid core of ice exists beneath the chandeliers, you don't have a prayer of getting in good ice screws. Often, if you can just hold it together through a stretch of dicey chandeliers, you'll find better ice where you can place protection—but not always, so don't count on it. Because of the fragile nature of chandelier ice, if you can't find good pro, tool testing is your best defense against falling. One nice thing about chandeliers is that you can often kick your boots in several inches to create good footholds. If the temperature is warm, though, it's best to just walk away.

Bouldering around the start of a new route in Val d'Prohibition, Italy, I was on some nasty, warm chandelier ice. Quicker than I could say *merde*, one tool sheared, then the other. I landed in a stream at the base of the route, and sheepishly crawled out of the water. Fortunately for me, my new Italian friends pretended not to notice.

*If you can't get purchase in a sheet of chandelier ice, you may be able to find a natural hole, push your axe through and toggle it sideways.*

## ROTTEN ICE

Rotten ice is just that—rotten. Ice deteriorates during warm temperatures and under direct sunshine, and if the heat spell is prolonged, you get rotten ice. You can also get rotten ice when snowpack and ice are mixed in the flow. At best, rotten ice covers only the surface; you can burrow down to solid ice. At worst, rotten ice is the consistency of porridge—and even less appetizing. You'll know when you encounter rotten ice.

If you have only a short stretch of rotten ice, it may be worth persevering. An adze that's designed to be planted in hard snow or rotten ice can help here, but you'll probably wish you had two—maybe you can borrow the adze tool of your second? If the ice is only a little rotten, it may be reasonable to climb—but don't trust your ice protection. On the first pitch of *Wowie Zowie* in Valdez, Alaska, the first 90 feet were sun baked and rotten. I didn't bother to place protection through this stretch, but instead used my energy and psyche to keep climbing safely, testing my placements and kicking good footholds. The first screw, placed in the rotten ice, was terrible. Fortunately, the last six screws in the 250-foot pitch found solid ice.

If the ice is medium rotten, you can get by, but it's probably not worth it. Many years ago on the south-facing *Glenwood Falls* in Colorado, I deemed the ice too rotten to climb. My less experienced partner had different ideas, and after all, we had driven all this way. He coerced me into the lead. The whole way up the first pitch I envisioned my tools ripping out—I was terrified, expecting to hit the deck at any moment. I didn't, of course, or you'd be reading this book written by some other punter. That was the last time I let myself be pressured by my partner into a dangerous lead.

On *Gravity's Rainbow* in Ouray, Colorado, we found ice so rotten it wouldn't even hold our tools. Just as well that we

*Heel hooking helps you keep your balance on thin icicles.*

couldn't get off the ground. If it's warm enough for ice to be this rotten, expect things to start falling down. Head home and drink a cold one.

## SMALL PILLARS

Climbing a tiny pillar, a body-width or so in circumference, demands brute strength and delicate technique. Even a small pillar can squash you like a bug if you bring it down—not to mention that you'll probably hit the ground. Plant your picks with dainty pecks, lightly tapping them to get a placement. Keep your picks staggered, to avoid fracturing the pillar. Don't kick the pillar, but rather set your front points onto the ice, or tap them in gently. Another technique that's light on the ice is to wrap your legs around the icicle and squeeze while you work your picks up. Ride 'em cowboy!

You can also heel hook around the back of a small pillar. You'll be happy to have heel points when using this technique. The sequence goes like this: lock off on your left arm, heel hook the right foot, and move the right tool high (delicately!). Now move the right foot up, gently front pointing, then the left foot, and stand up. Lock off on the right arm, and heel hook with the left foot. Move the left tool up, then the feet, stand up, lock off again, and repeat. You won't have too many moves of this—if the pillar is this thin, it's either short, or it thickens very soon, or you'll knock it down for sure. If the pillar is truly thin, don't bother with protection until you get to the thick stuff. It won't hold you anyway, and it may break the whole pillar down.

Sharp front points and picks are critical on small pillars. I once tried to climb a tiny, cold, brittle pillar in Valpelline, Italy, with dull picks. After two moves, I was sure I'd knock the pillar off, so I stepped back down. Later, armed with scalpel-sharp picks, I scratched my way up the pillar, squeezing my legs around the pillar like an Anaconda crushing its prey. I tapped the sharp, thin picks into the pillar; the difference between them and the dull picks was incredible. The pillar didn't fall down.

## HANGING PILLARS

Climbing a hanging pillar—a giant white fang suspended from the lip of a roof—is one of the most exhilarating and dangerous endeavors in pure ice climbing. You often crank wild mixed moves out of a rock roof just to reach a hanging pillar. Brutish, overhanging rock climbing leads to delicate, vertical ice climbing—a splendid contrast in techniques.

What makes hanging pillars so precarious is the fact that they're hanging free, unsupported at the bottom—tons of ice suspended only by the bonds in the ice. Because of the stress created by this weight, one tool placement in the wrong spot brings the whole thing down—with you on it! Many big-name ice climbers—including Alex Lowe, Stevie Haston, Mark Wilford and Francois Damilamo—have taken a big ride when the pillars they were on snapped. Miraculously, they all walked away. Some of these guys have more lives than a cat. Don't think that you'll be so lucky. It's a good bet that if you break off a big pillar, you'll be killed. As John Sherman pointed out when he reviewed this book, for every ice climbing miracle, there are several fatalities.

Exiting a well protected rock roof onto a hanging icicle. Get your feet in the icicle as soon as possible.

I've never been keen to ride a collapsing pillar. My first try on *Octopussy* in Vail, I spied a horizontal crack all the way across the pillar, just below the rock line. No way, not today! I bailed. Returning a week later, the crack was still there, but the pillar hadn't broken. I figured the ice must have re-fused. Still, I let Stevie Haston test it first. Stevie gave me some wise advice: keep your picks set loosely in their holes, so if the pillar does come down, you can get free and jump clear.

In addition, it's unwise to place screws too early in a hanging pillar. When *Suffer Machine's* pillar in the Canadian Rockies broke loose with Rafael Slawinski on it, his ice screws kept him fastened to the plunging pillar. When the pillar hit the ground, it broke up, and thankfully, Rafael's screws came free. He ended up dangling from his ropes, rather than being sucked through his carabiners. This was another disaster averted by pure luck.

When I tried *Virtual Reality* in the Rockies with Topher Donahue, the final pitch was a 40-foot-long, free hanging pillar— 2 feet from touching down at the bottom. The temperatures had been warm for several days. I badly wanted to climb this thing, and I tried to feel good about it, but I couldn't convince myself. Despite Topher's encouragement, we bailed. Topher was wise enough to trust my judgement, and not let a competitive urge send him up the death pillar. We never made it back to *Virtual Reality*, but we learned that three days later the pillar had touched down, and another party climbed it. Patience will keep you safe, and persistence will get you up these ephemeral routes.

If the water flow takes a broader path across the lip of a roof, you can get a hanging sheet of ice rather than a hanging pillar. We confronted such a dangling sheet on the first ascent of *Cuore di Pietro, Cuore di Ghiaccio (Heart of Stone, Heart of Ice)* in Valeille, Italy. Starting up the overhanging, thin ice, a super-dull pick ripped out and I was left dangling by one arm. (Dumb, I should have known better.) After changing the pick, I reached the rock roof behind the ice. Here I chopped a good stance so I could sew up the roof with protection, while my belayer, Rudy Buccella, shivered. After placing several pieces in the rotten rock, I dry tooled to the back of the ice sheet. My original plan was to downclimb the ice sheet, climb under its bottom, and reemerge on the front side. But when I got to the back side, I had a better idea. I chopped a 2-foot-diameter hole, and crawled through the ice sheet. Immediately, I went from pumping out a scary rock roof, to sitting in an ice hole, resting and laughing.

## THIN ICE

Ice comes in varying degrees of thickness, from big, fat pillars to thin coatings of verglas. When ice becomes too thin to accept full-length ice screws, protection and tool placements become precarious. If you have the right attitude and technique, though, it's amazing what you can climb with just a scant layer of ice smearing the rock.

Thin ice is reasonable to climb only when the temperatures are near or slightly below freezing. Warm, thin ice becomes poorly bonded to the underlying rock, and when this happens, the ice holds little weight. If you have to climb a short section of warm, flaky, boilerplate ice, the best bet may be to clear it away and dry tool the rock beneath; or climb like you're walking on china plates, because that's essentially what you're doing.

Super-cold conditions can also be problematic with thin ice, because the ice may chip off when you try to scratch out a placement. Often, it's a fine line. Before the first ascent of *Sea of Vapors*, Bruce Hendricks backed off because cold conditions made the ultra-thin ice too fragile. Warmer temperatures a few days later allowed "reasonable" pick placements in the plastic ice, and he made the first ascent of this WI7+ testpiece with Joe Josephson.

Along with temperatures, rock type can affect the bonding of thin ice. Limestone is more porous than granite, so ice tends to bond better to it. Because of this, frightfully thin ice over limestone can sometimes be climbed in conditions that would be impossible on granite.

Climbing well-bonded thin ice often feels like rock climbing. You can't bury a pick anywhere you want, so you have to scope the ice to

*You want to be delicate when climbing a thin ice sheet.*

*This ice slab has meltwater running behind, and it's incredibly fragile.*

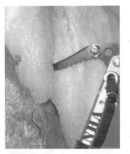

*Thin ice can provide good purchase for your picks, provided it's bonded well to the rock.*

find the best placements, and adjust your technique to accommodate the existing holds. Often, a long reach stretches from one hold to the next. Other times, it's a series of dicey little moves.

Above all, thin ice requires a delicate approach—you must make careful use of what little ice you have. A Neanderthal approach will leave you staring at dry rock and dull picks. When the going gets thin, peck the picks and tap the front points lightly to create little divots to hook and stand on, and to avoid destroying the ice. Often, you can place the picks at an oblique angle, so you get three or four teeth into the ice rather than one or two. Gently test thin ice placements, move delicately, distribute your weight between tools and crampons, and keep your feet and picks still. The thinner the ice, the more important these refinements of technique become.

The worst thin-ice condition is verglas—ice that's thick enough to obscure the rock and make it hideously slick, yet barely thick enough to set a pick in. Even with verglas conditions, though, ice is rarely uniformly thin. It usually forms smears of varying thickness, with occasional puddles of thicker ice, and barren patches of rock. When climbing verglas, read the rock underneath. Set the picks and crampons on small edges and in tiny cracks of the underlying rock like you're dry tooling, and search for patches of thicker ice where you can set the picks. Ice often collects inside cracks or above a small ledge, for example.

Often you'll combine the techniques of ice climbing, thin ice, and dry tooling. Versatility, creativity, and constant awareness of what your tools and feet are doing, as well as poise, confidence and balance, are critical here. Frequently, thin ice is found on slabs, and the techniques and posture of a slab climber come into play.

*Kevin Cooper mixing it up on Necrophilia in Rocky Mountain National Park.* TOPHER DONAHUE PHOTO

Classic mixed climbing—one tool and one foot on rock, the others on ice.

Stemming and crossing arms to take advantage of the natural holds.

Chimneying between the rock and the back of the icicle makes for easy climbing.

As ice reaches 3 or 4 inches thick, you can loosen up somewhat on the technique, but protection will still be difficult. Careful movement and ferreting out protection opportunities may carry you up the pitch.

Protection may be sketchy to nonexistent on a thin-ice route, and it might be desperate or impossible to bail. If protection is bad, downclimbing may be your only way out if you stall. Size up the route carefully before you commit to it, and don't bite off more than you can chew. See Chapter 7 for coverage of thin ice protection.

## MIXED CLIMBING

One hand jamming a crack, one tool stuck in an ice wart, one foot stemming rock, the other front pointing a smear—nothing tests a climber's cool head and all-around skill like mixed climbing. The possibilities are endless—take all the moves you can do rock climbing, plus all the moves you can do ice climbing, throw in dry tooling, add the protection possibilities of rock and ice, and you get mixed climbing. A solid foundation in rock climbing and ice climbing techniques, combined with a creative sense of how to mix them up, are prerequisites to success.

Mixed routes run the gamut from ice routes with a bit of rock to rock routes with a bit of ice. If the route has a good deal of ice, climb the ice as much as possible, and use the rock to supplement the available ice. As the ice becomes thinner and more scarce, the rock becomes the primary medium. Every climb is different, and a given climb may change drastically in a few days, or a few hours.

### Dry Tooling

Dry tooling is simply rock climbing, using your picks and crampons for purchase rather than fingers and rock shoes. It's amazing the tiny dimples you can hold onto with the steely points of your picks, but try to smear a sloper and you'll be skatin'.

Mono-point crampons work great for standing on tiny rock divots.

Scratch marks on the rock from dry tooling. This is why you shouldn't practice in an established rock climbing or bouldering area.

The shape of the pick is critical—if you don't ramp the end of the pick as shown in Chapter 2, it won't hold well on flat edges. When dry tooling, you have an amazing number of options. You can hook the pick on an edge, divot, or small crack, or lay it sideways across an edge; you can hook the adze on an edge, torque it in a crack, or set it in a crack and layback off it; you can jam the hammerhead in a crack like a nut, and some hammerheads will hook an edge; and you can cam the shaft in a deep crack. Some climbers even bolt a sky hook on the head of the axe for hooking small edges.

Once you set the pick, weight it slowly to make sure it'll hold. As you move, keep the pick still so it doesn't sketch off. Be careful not to move too high on a placement, or the pick may skate. Practice dry tooling beforehand so you'll have confidence when the moment of truth arrives. However, picks and crampons put hideous scratches on the rock, so don't practice in everyone's favorite bouldering area, or at a classic crag. Instead, find an obscure, out-of-the-way piece of rock to work out your tricks. You can even practice in a rock gym (your own) by placing tape on the picks and using rock shoes. This will help you learn the art of moving on your tools. For safety, remove the adze, and pad hammer heads with foam and tape while you practice.

Sometimes, rather than dry tooling, it's better to holster the tools, or dangle them from your wrists, and grab the holds with your hands. Thin gloves help here, and sometimes you may even do a pitch, or a few moves, without gloves. Of course, you probably won't do this during an arctic blast.

Because mixed routes involve standing on thin ice and rock, many climbers prefer mono-point crampons for their superior sensitivity and precision. The key, as in delicate rock climbing, is to hold your feet steady when the points are placed on small holds—any movement may send a foot sketching. Usually you'll set the front points on edges, divots, or in tiny cracks. If you have a large edge, you can flat foot to reduce the strain on your calves.

*Hooking the pick on a rock edge.*

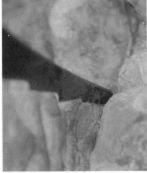

*Hooking in a tiny crack can be amazingly secure.*

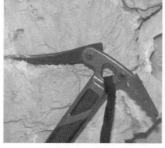

Turning the tool sideways can allow you to get more of the pick on a hold, which sometimes adds stability to the placement.

Picks jam great in thin cracks, as long as the crack tapers a little.

Hooking a large rock edge. The visor helps protect your face in case the pick pops.

1. The lobotomy move on rock. A bad idea.

2. You can cam the adze across a crack for purchase.

1. Some adzes work well for holding a rock edge.

2. Jamming a tight crack with the adze.

1. You can even undercling a crack with your adze.

2. Liebacking with the pick in one hand, and the adze in the other.

The adze cammed across a mucky hand-size crack.

Sometimes it's best to holster the tools, remove the gloves, and climb freehanded.

1. Liebacking off the adze, and jamming the pick.

2. Rock protection is often essential gear on mixed pitches.

1. As in rock climbing, suck your hips in when approaching a roof.

2. Micro-stem with the feet and suck the hips in to get weight off the arms.

Steve House on the
rarely formed third
pitch of Virtual
Reality, Alberta.
JOE JOSEPHSON PHOTO

Will Gadd gettin' pro
in Spiceboy, Boulder
Canyon, Colorado.
TOPHER DONAHUE PHOTO

# Leading

Leading ice requires ultimate control. With 24 points on your feet, an adze, pick, and spike in each hand, and sharp ice screws on your rack, you run a good chance of getting skewered in a fall, or catching your crampons in the ice and breaking an ankle, tibia, and/or fibula—so falling is usually a bad idea. Besides that, protection in less-than-perfect ice may rip out as you plunge headlong down the icefall. We're not trying to scare potential ice climbers away, but rather inform them that leading ice is serious business!

## IS THE ICE SAFE?

The first consideration when approaching an ice climb is whether or not the route is "safe". Safety must be evaluated on many levels: Is the approach safe? Is the area *surrounding* the climb safe? Is the ice good enough to give solid protection, and is the difficulty of the climb within the skill of the climbing team? All these issues must be addressed.

Last April, on a photo shoot for this book, I hoped to photograph mixed climbing on Vail's *Seventh Tentacle*, a climb behind the famous and spectacular freestanding *Fang*. On the approach we noticed a large crack at the top of the *Fang*. When we got to *Seventh Tentacle*, we saw huge blocks of ice hanging near the crack, above our proposed route. We bailed to a safer area. On the hike out we looked up to see the upper portion of the *Fang* missing. Had we stayed in the area, my wife, climbing guide Dan Gambino, and I would have been pulverized. Another climber at *Glenwood Falls* in Colorado wasn't so lucky. A Volkswagen-Beetle-sized chunk of ice broke free, smashing the life out of this poor man. Two other friends of mine met their demise in separate incidents when avalanches poured over their routes, washing them away to eternity.

The moral: always inspect the terrain above for hanging icicles and avalanche slopes. If you see dangerous danglers, particularly if it's warm, run away. Rapid temperature drops can be destabilizing, because they cause shrinkage and compression in the ice. If you decide to stay, avoid being below these things. Likewise with avalanche slopes.

Also, check the quality of the ice. Is it solid, and well bonded? Does the prospect for good protection seem likely? Does the ice look within your capabilities? Is it similar to what you've seen before? Progress to harder ice leads should be made in small, incremental steps, rather than leaps and bounds. We have 13-year-olds that can lead 5.12 sport routes in a few months, but the judgement and experience required to safely lead WI5 and 6 merits a much longer apprenticeship. Also, as mentioned before, don't be suckered by grades. It might say WI4 in the guide book, but it might be in WI7 condition.

Another ice hazard to beware of, particularly during prolonged warm spells, or in late season, is the hollow tube—a veneer of ice that resembles a pillar, but is actually a fragile soda straw with water pouring down the inside. On a late-season solo of the *Rigid Designator*, I became terrified near the top when my tool punched a large hole through the suddenly thin shell of ice. Without warning I was staring 100 feet down into the bowels of the *Designator*, watching a raging waterfall. Delicate, deliberate maneuvering granted me salvation. Chris Archer wasn't so lucky. Leading *Marble Falls*, he plunged into the hollow tube when its veneer broke. Trapped in the freezing water, he had only minutes to react. Quick thinking, a strong will to live, and luck saved Chris—he valiantly chopped a tunnel through the ice and freed himself.

See Chapter 9 for a more comprehensive discussion of ice climbing hazards.

## PRACTICE LEAD

It's wise to start off slowly on your first leads. First, make a couple of "practice leads," setting protection and clipping a rope like a normal lead, but with a toprope, so you can get the feel of leading, without the danger. If possible, have an experienced ice climber or guide clean the pitch to evaluate your protection. Once you feel comfortable on the practice leads, go for the real thing. Choose a route well below your toproping ability, and place ice screws frequently (every 5 to 8 feet). Placing more protection than you need keeps you safe while you work out your leading system, and provides good practice for firing in pro.

After these first few leads, slowly step up the difficulty. Be willing to bail if conditions are bad or if things don't feel right.

## STRATEGY

Before climbing, study the route and pick a good line. Look for solid ice, out of any major water drips. Seek grooves and the outside edges of pillars where you can stem, or small ledges where you can easily place protection. Try to find ice caves or protected ledges for the belays. On popular routes, follow the line of existing pick holes to make the climbing easier—unless, of course, you're seeking out difficulty. Estimate how many ice screws you'll need, and throw in a couple extra—don't forget about the belays. If the line has exposed rock, toss in rock gear as well. Choosing the optimal rack, without getting weighed down, is the goal.

Find a belay stance that's safe from hanging icicles and debris knocked down by the leader. **Never climb beneath another party.** If the belay is exposed, set a bombproof belay anchor. If the belayer's on the ground, and it's relatively flat, forget the anchor—it's better if the belayer can dodge falling ice, provided you trust him or her not to trip over his feet and pull you off the pitch (some climbers disagree on this point, thinking that the belayer should always be anchored).

Now, the moment of truth: tie in, double check all safety systems, and cast off. If you're leading just above the ground, climb up as far as you feel comfortable, like 10 to 20 feet (sometimes more, sometimes less, depending on the difficulty), and set the first piece of protection. When you're leading from a belay above the ground, it's better to put good protection in immediately above the belay, to decrease the fall factor and bolster the belay anchors (see Chapter 7 for an important discussion of fall factors).

It's good to have a game plan regarding your protection. For example, say you have four 22-centimeter screws, two stubbies (10 centimeters), and six 17-centimeter screws on the rack. You might always set one of the long screws at the belay, coupled with a 17-centimeter screw. The first piece in the pitch also gets a long screw, as does the ledge midway up the pitch where you can easily hang out. In the crux pillar, you set the two brand-new 17-centimeter screws, because they're sharp and they go in fast. In the thin section you fire in one stubbie, and at the end of the pitch, when you're pumped, you set the other stubbie just below the bulge, to get you through the last move. The variations and options here are many. The main idea is to have a plan, and creatively solve the protection needs of the pitch.

As you progress up the pitch, constantly evaluate the quality of the ice and the quality of your protection. If things are getting out of hand—bad ice, bad pro, and/or bad head—bail out while you still can. See Chapter 8 for more on retreating.

## LEADING SYSTEMS

Many systems exist for leading ice, setting protection, and dealing with ice tools. It's good to try different systems to see what works best for you. Above all, keep things simple.

Some climbers tether both tools to their harness, with cords and slings crossing every which way. This may add some safety, especially for new ice climbers; but it also makes ice climbing unnecessarily complex. Tethers tangle in your rack and climbing rope. If you use a tether, a good system is to stretch shock cord through the center of 0.5-inch or 9/16-inch tubular webbing, so the webbing retracts and doesn't hang too low, but also extends to accommodate your maximum reach.

Once you gain confidence you can ditch the tethers to simplify life on the sharp end. As the ice gets steeper, well-designed leashes become increasingly important. With good leashes, good technique, and self-control, tethers become more of a distraction than a helpful piece of gear.

On lead, carrying a third tool can save the day if you drop or break a tool. Ice climbers used to religiously carry a third tool, but now, many climbers forgo the spare to save weight. Not smart. If you're on a big, fat flow, you could always set a screw and bail if you break a tool. On hard mixed terrain, or precarious ice structures, where you might not get a piece to bail from, the

*Carrying a third tool when you're leading ice is a good idea in case you break a pick or drop a tool. It's especially important on poorly protected pitches where you can't easily bail out if something goes wrong. If you don't carry a third tool, at least carry a spare pick and a wrench to change it (and hope you never break a shaft or drop a tool). This climber has a short hammer as a backup tool.*

loss of a tool without a backup could be your demise—carry a spare. On long routes, the team can bring a single spare tool for the leader to carry. Most everyone who reviewed this book agreed that the third tool is essential gear for the leader, and that leaving the third tool at home is not a smart place to save weight.

## THE RACK

How much protection should you bring? It really depends on how long the pitches are and how often you place gear. Do a little math. "If I place three screws at a belay, and lead 150 feet with pro every 15 feet, then set three screws at the next belay, we'll need 15 screws, maybe 16 for good measure." Sixteen screws would be quite a large rack. With experience you can get by with two good screws at a belay, and perhaps run out some of the easier sections, so a total of ten or twelve screws and pound-ins usually suffices, but remember, that only leaves you with six to eight for leading on a multi-pitch route. If your strategy involves extra-long pitches, you'll need extra screws. Expecting thin ice? Better toss in some ice hooks and stubbies. If rock placements are available, throw in some cams, wired nuts and pitons. And don't forget the Screamers.

You can rack the pro on a gear sling, or the racking loops of your harness. Sometimes, when encumbered in winter clothes, it's hard to get gear off a sling, because it hangs behind your back. Being right-handed, I carry most of my screws, racked two or three to a carabiner, on my right hip. The carabiners are oriented with the gates opening down and out, and I tuck my jacket in under the harness so it doesn't impede my access to the rack. To easily remove a screw, I push the gate open with the screw's hanger. I also put a few quickdraws on the right hip, so I can easily place and clip protection with my right hand. To balance the load, I'll hang some less urgent gear on my left hip. I

A rack organized on the hip.

A mixed rack.

The Simond racking rig carries a few ice screws, and makes it easy to remove them.

also rack rock pro by urgency, using the front of the harness for quick access, and the back of the harness or a gear sling for distributing the load. Shoulder and double-length slings are twisted up, clipped to a carabiner, and carried on my harness, so I don't have to fight pulling the slings off over my helmet and tools. But this is my system. You might find that something different works better for you, so don't be afraid to experiment.

## Hints for Successful Racking

*by* Kim Csizmazia

I remember my first ice lead. It was in Maple Canyon and I was in a bad mood. My ex was using our rack for an ambitious first ascent. I was nervous and wanted the gear to be familiar, so I felt that I deserved to use the rack. This was, after all, my first lead. Peevish, I grabbed Kennan Harvey's rack and stomped to the base of *Cobble Cruncher*. As I racked I noticed that some of the screws were still full of ice. Irritated, I knocked the screws on the side of a cobble.

"Don't hit the screws on the rock, you'll dull them, and settle down already," scolded my friend and climbing mentor Topher Donahue. Now I was also irritated at myself for being an idiot. My friend Beth belayed me. As I tied in I vented to her about the scrappy nature of Kennan's rack. Fifty feet up I was finally calm and focused. There was no other option. I clipped D-shaped carabiners with gloves, drove dull screws left-handed, and dropped a Spectre. All my angst melted, and I was in love with ice climbing.

When racking, bring enough gear to safely protect the climb. An insufficient rack may lead to dangerous runouts or a good excuse to back off. Neither are good options for me. Experiment with many different ways of racking. Learn from others and expand on their ideas. Be flexible and keep an open mind, but before a hard lead, rack with purpose. Know why you have racked the way you have.

On a long mixed pitch, I rack my gear on a Black Diamond Zodiac gear sling, so I can throw the rack on over my coat, and because I like racking loops on both sides of my body. Gear often gets lost under my coat paunch when it's on my harness. I might carry a full rack of cams up to #3 Camalot, racked from small to large on one side, and on the other side I'll put my TCUs, stoppers, RPs, Tricams, and five or so assorted pins. I rack my screws on my harness in the rear loops to keep their sharp teeth off of my thigh when I high step. I face the screws in the same direction, hanging so the teeth face back, and the racking carabiner opening down and out so the screws are easy to unclip and reclip. I put stubbies (short, 10-centimeter screws) on one side, and 17-centimeter screws on the other, with a couple of 22s (long screws) in the very back. I also carry Spectres, racked through the eye, with the beak facing back.

Quickdraws go on the front loops of my harness for easy accessibility. A variety of lengths works best for equalizing and preventing rope drag. I also carry a few Screamers. Shoulder-length slings are essential, especially for equalizing. I throw them over my shoulder, each with one carabiner. I carry a total of 12 to 15 quickdraws and slings, and a cordelette.

Once you're leading, pay attention, be creative, and study the ice. Keep in mind that no one ever died by putting in too much gear. Take pride in a well-protected climb. If you find yourself in deep with a tangled cluster of gear and bulky gloves, I've found that a loud bellow of obscenities often helps sort things out.

## PROTECTING THE LEAD

Placing and removing ice screws is a drag; it consumes time and energy, and interrupts the flow of climbing. And it's often the crux of the climb. But nothing calms the mind like solid protection, and staying calm is crucial for efficient, safe climbing. How frequently to set pro depends on your experience and style, as well as the ice conditions, steepness, availability of pro, quality of the protection below and urgency of the situation. Once you get up to speed you might run 15 feet or more between screws. Always keep an eye out for rock or natural protection options that may be easier to get than an ice screw.

On long routes you might need to run the pro out a bit to avoid a frigid bivi. Don't hesitate to use an ice screw whenever you need one, but in the mountains speed is safety. When you do run it out, control is essential. *Control will keep you alive.* Move only on solid placements, because your axes are your immediate belay. The previous sentence is important to ponder and understand. Once you accept the concept of tools as your immediate, or portable belay, you can also understand the idea of moving the least bomber tool first, to keep the best part of your portable belay intact.

*Ezio Marlier, detached from his tool while placing protection on Il Regalo, Val díAosta, Italy.*

Let the ice and the formations dictate where you place pro. Keep an open mind, and look for good ice and good stances. If the flow is thick, solid, and well frozen, you can set an ice screw or pound-in almost anywhere. I often protect when I find an energy-saving stance, and run it out when the going is hard. Of course, on a 100-foot vertical pillar you'll have to place some gear from difficult stances. Here, try to at least stem to get some weight off your arms, and fire the gear in fast. Take the time to find the optimal rest position to place gear from. Don't forget to place protection for the second at the beginnings of traverses and after the hard moves on traverses, so you don't set them up for a pendulum fall.

Also remember that as soon as you climb past a ledge or cauliflower, it's as if you're near the ground again—take a short fall, and SNAP!, compound fracture. Keep these features in mind when deciding where to place protection.

If the ice is chandeliered, rotten, or slushy, find the most solid places for your ice screws. Often a horizontal break at the base of a pillar (large or small) has good ice. In this case, it's usually best to place the ice screw or pound-in straight down into the ice. Otherwise, test the ice with your picks to find a solid patch of ice. Blue, green, or yellow ice is usually solid; white ice often contains air bubbles or pockets, which decrease the strength of the ice. Avoid tunnel vision—look around until you find a good spot for protection.

The strength of an ice anchor depends on the placement and the quality of the ice. A good screw can hold more than 4,000 pounds, and a good ice hook 1,800 pounds, but a bad placement may not hold your rucksack. Strength and nuances of setting ice anchors are covered in Chapter 7.

Sometimes you want to set the protection as high as possible, especially if you're leaving a good stance and casting off onto a stretch of hard climbing. Ice screws with a coffee grinder handle are fairly easy to place above your head (as are pound-ins). As before, clear the bad surface ice, start the hole with your pick, and insert the screw, maintaining inward pressure until the threads bite.

Now crank the screw in fast and clip it. This climber has chosen to let his ice axe dangle from the wrist loop so he never detaches from his tools.

### Setting an Ice Screw

Ideally you'll find solid ice just above waist level in which to place the screw. This way you can easily apply inward pressure on the screw. I usually place screws with my favored hand, but it's

1. Placing an ice screw on lead. Find a flat or concave spot where the ice looks solid, with no air pockets. Set one axe (the axe in the non screw-placing hand) very securely, high enough so you can hang straight-armed from it. Clear the rotten surface ice where you're placing the screw by aggressively bashing it away with your other tool. Flatten out an area 10 inches in diameter.

2. Make a starter hole for your screw with the pick of your axe.

3. Set the screw. It's usually easier to place an ice screw at chest-to-waistt level, rather than above your head. Here the leader is using a detachable leash system; after starting the screw hole, he set the axe solidly above and detached his wrist loop.

4. Now quickly turn the screw in. Keep a fair amount of inward pressure on the screw to get it started, but once the threads bite you can forego the inward pressure and just turn the screw.

5. Near the end, bumps in the ice that you failed to clear often prevent the hanger from turning, so you may have to grab the axe again to clear them.

6. Now tighten the screw to the hilt and clip in. Ahhhhh, what a relief. This screw is clipped with a Screamer, a load-limiting quickdraw. More on these later. Relax for a moment, and carry on.

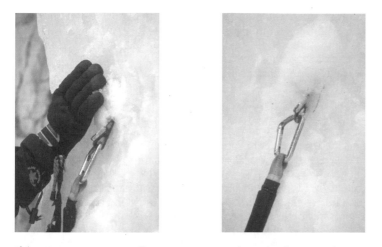

*If the air temperature is really warm—or worse, the sun is shining on the screws—they'll melt out fairly quickly. If possible, pack snow over the screw.*

important to be somewhat ambidextrous in case you need to place with the other hand. Clear rotten or brittle ice from the surface and create a flat spot about 10 inches in diameter. Spend as much time as necessary to get to good ice—your life may depend on it. This is no time to be lazy. In the center of the clearing, chop a hole 2 or so inches deep with your pick, ideally the same diameter as your ice screw. Creating the starter hole is also crucial to setting screws efficiently—don't shortcut this step either.

Now set the screw in the hole, and turn it until the hanger comes flush with the ice. A dull or inferior ice screw may need a few taps from the hammer before the teeth bite to pull it in. Usually pushing a sharp screw into the ice during the first few half-turns gets the threads started—unless the ice is horribly hard and brittle. Once the threads bite, you can stop pushing in and just turn the screw.

Evaluate the piece as you set it. Watch that no cracks shoot from it, or dinner plates form around it. If the ice does plate, clear the newly fractured ice and keep driving the screw into the same hole. If this happens, clear more ice with your pick and set the anchor deeper in the same spot. Make sure the screw encounters resistance all the way in and doesn't hit any big air pockets. Sometimes you'll feel a small air pocket, then the screw will hit solid ice again (you'll feel new resistance). Provided the air pocket isn't too big, these placements can be okay. Experience will help you evaluate these screws.

Warm temperatures and direct sunshine can partially melt out your ice screws. If possible, pack snow over screws exposed to sunlight and warm air.

## What Angle?

Contrary to three decades of conventional wisdom, ice screws with high relief threads are strongest when screwed 15 to 20 degrees *below* a line perpendicular to the ice. However, in melt-out conditions, rotten ice, or when using pound-ins with low-relief threads, angle the screws 15 to 20 degrees *above* the perpendicular line. See Chapter 7 for more discussion on the best angle for ice screws.

## What Length

Many climbers use stubbies (10-centimeter screws) to save energy when placing protection. While these can be very strong in perfect ice, they should not substitute for medium (17-centimeter) or long (22-centimeter) screws for protecting a lead, especially in less than perfect ice. At the beginning of a pitch, with little rope out, the force of a lead fall is at its highest, so it's important to place longer screws. Likewise for belay anchors—you want the maximum strength. Also, if the ice is rotten or aerated, long screws are the way to go—the longer the better. Far up the pitch, however, with a lot of rope out, the force of a fall is much less. Here you might get away with shorter screws—if the ice is good. Still, personally I consider stubbies as a tool for thin ice only, and that's where I'll use them. Modern, sharp screws go in pretty fast. After I've spent the time and energy to locate a spot, clear it, create a starter hole, and start the screw, I'll go ahead and zip the extra 7 centimeters of screw in to have a 17-centimeter screw over a stubbie.

## Free Climbing

Many systems exist for setting lead protection. A wise ice climber once said, "the only bad style is falling. The only ethic is speed." John Sherman added, "I prefer pure style, but not enough to die for it. Dying is really bad style." That said, the purest style for leading ice is to place the ice screws from free stances, hanging from your hands rather than your harness. On moderate ice it's easy to set pro from free stances, but on steep ice it requires effort. Find the most restful free stance available, stemming or flat footing if possible. Avoid awkward or strenuous stances—even if you have to climb up a couple more moves. Plant the tool in your weaker hand high and solid, so you can hang straight-armed from it. Now set the screw with your favored hand quickly and decisively, clip it, rest a minute if you got pumped, and move on.

Sometimes the ice near your favored arm is bad, and you'll place an ice screw with your weaker hand. It's good to practice this beforehand, so when it counts, you're not fumbling around to set pro.

When placing the screw, you have two options for dealing with your ice tool. You can set it in the ice and detach from it, or you can let it dangle from your wrist. Some wrist leashes easily detach from the tool. If you don't have one of these, simply remove your hand from the leash. Some climbers remove their hand from their leash and mitten, leaving the mitt hanging in the wrist leash, so they can place gear barehanded. Whenever

*This climber isn't using detachable wrist leashes, but she has freed her hand from the wrist leash to place a screw.*

1. After he sets the screw and clips it, the axe will be hanging from his wrist.

2. With a little practice, you can learn to flip the axe up . . .

3. . . . and catch it near the bottom of the shaft.

4. Now reposition your hand so you're gripping the axe where you want it.

you detach from the tool, make sure it's well planted, so you can't lose it. Also, plant it far enough away from the screw so you don't bump it while setting the screw. If you dangle the tool from your wrist, flip it up and catch it in your hand when you're done placing pro.

Some climbers gain temporary protection when setting screws by draping one of their double ropes over a solidly planted tool. At least one tool has a specially designed groove to cradle the rope. I'd definitely avoid falling on this setup, and I'd never use it if the exposed top edge of the pick was sharpened for easy removal, because it might slice your rope. Clipping the rope into the spike or wrist loop of a well-planted tool is more secure, but it's a hassle. One friend of mine clips the rope into a draw placed in the spike of his free tool. Then he sets the screw, and unclips the draw from his axe and clips it into the screw, with the rope already attached.

Tethers connecting the tools to your harness, as discussed above, also keep you backed up while setting protection. The most pure style, though, is to be solid enough to fire in good gear, clip it, and move on.

## Setting a Pound-in

Pound-ins were quite popular before easy-to-place ice screws appeared—the desperate leader could slam one home and breathe relief. The problem is, pound-ins can be hard to get started, and even tougher to remove. If placed in a tight space where the head can't turn, the second must chop away ice before removing the pound-in. Also, pound-ins can disturb fragile ice structures, or cause brittle ice to dinner plate. However, pound-ins are occasionally the easiest pro to set on lead, especially when you need to set the gear high. Leader security rules over

Pound-ins are easiest to place above your head because you can get a good swing to drive them home. Like always, first clear the rotten surface ice and make a good starter hole for the pound-in. Stab the screw into the starter hole hard enough to stick.

Tap the pound-in first to get it started, then pound it with hard, precise blows of your hammer.

Clip the pound-in, rest for a moment, and climb on.

the second's convenience, so if you want to set a pound-in, slam it home.

To place a pound-in, find some solid ice, ideally an arm's length above the shoulder of your favored hand. Clear away rotten surface ice and make a starting hole. Now stab the pound-in forcefully into the hole, so it stays in place. Tap the pound-in gently at first, so it doesn't rebound out of the hole and fall. Once started, drive it to the hilt. Listen for the pound-in to ring home bomber. Watch the ice carefully as you drive the pound-in, and beware of shearing dinner plates. Avoid setting pound-ins in tight spots where the head can't turn, or your partner will (rightfully) curse you.

### Cleaning Screws and Pound-ins

To remove a screw, unclip the rope and spin the hanger counterclockwise. If the screw won't turn, you can lever the hanger with the quickdraw carabiner (large carabiners help here) or pick of your ice axe to get it started, then finish with your fingers. To remove a pound-in, clear any ice that bars the hanger from turning, then tap the head two or more revolutions with a hammer. Finish by hand. You can also use the pick of an axe as a lever to twist out a pound-in.

Clear ice from the core of the screw immediately after removal by smacking it against the ice. Be careful not to damage the threads—smack the upper part of the screw. Also, don't scratch up the screw's interior by clearing it with your picks, or it'll become harder to clean in the future. In cold conditions you can melt the ice out with a lighter, or, dreadfully, put it in your jacket to thaw so you can get the ice plug out. If it's really warm, you might be able to blow the ice out. Don't try this when it's cold. First because it won't work, and second because you'll freeze your lips to the screw. If you won't be using the screw until the next climbing trip, you can let it thaw in a warm place. Otherwise, clear the screw before resetting it, or else you'll be trying to thump in a solid cylinder next time you try to set the screw.

## Hanging to Place Protection

The ultimate goal should be to free climb. It's certainly more pure and satisfying, and hanging on your tools does constitute aid. But as some climbers say, "Ice climbing is too cold for ethics." When the going gets desperate some climbers hang from a tool to set protection. This technique breaks the lead into a series of shorter "pitches," allowing the rested leader to calmly and safely negotiate each run to the next protection. Cleaning a pitch led with this technique can be a chore, because many screws will be in the worst places to hang out.

*Here the climber has clipped the rope to the spike hole of his axe and he's getting tension from the belayer so he can easily place protection.*

Several methods for hanging to place protection exist. You can clip your rope into the spike or wrist leash of a well-placed tool and get tension from the belayer. Quicker, but less safe, you can drape one of your ropes over a tool. Grip the rope in your hand to gain tension, or have your belayer hold tension on the rope. Hanging from a tool like this is creepy, especially if the belayer doesn't hold you perfectly tight. Never do this if the sharpened, top edge of the pick is exposed, or you might shred your rope.

Another system, fairly popular in Europe, involves tethering your harness to one or both tools with a cam-locking sling that can be quickly tightened for tension. When it's time to hang and place protection, plant the tools well, tighten the slings on your harness, sit onto the tools and place your protection. This trick could be spoiled by ice freezing the cam-lock, the tethers getting tangled in your ropes and slings, or the tools popping if they're not planted well enough.

To rig a fifi for hanging, carry it attached to your harness with 18-or-so inches of extension, and tuck it into your harness so it doesn't tangle in your rack. When you need to place protection, set one tool **very** securely. Flip the fifi through the spike of the axe, or clip it to a loop on the wrist leash. Then sit back and relax (if you can relax with the loaded axe's spike pointing at your crotch). Don't move around; this may loosen the axe you're hanging from. Now place your protection, clip it, rest, and climb on. Note: this is not free climbing.

If you're too pumped to safely place protection, a fifi hook can provide some relief.

You can also rig a tether or two with tubular webbing. To keep the tether out of your way, thread the inside of the webbing with a shorter piece of bungee cord. Adjust the lengths so the tether stretches to full arm's length, and sucks up out of the way when the tool is close to your body.

A simpler system is to girth hitch a fifi hook onto your harness with a foot or two of extension—a carabiner can be used if a fifi isn't available. Keep the fifi tucked in your harness when it's not in use. To hang from your harness and set pro, hook the fifi into the spike hole or wrist leash of a well-placed axe.

For extra security you can tether your harness to one tool. Plant this tool solidly as a backup, then set the other tool and hang from it with the fifi. Now pull out your third tool and place the screw. Set bomber axe placements if you hang from them because they're spring-loaded, with the spike aimed straight toward your crotch.

Even if you never hang to place protection, you might rig a "panic sling" to your harness when pushing your limits. This way, if you get too pumped to think straight, you can quickly clip or fifi the sling to your tool and hang to sort things out.

Here, I must add that I personally strive to never hang on my tools during the pitch, but if I had a choice between hanging or falling, I'd definitely hang. I must also admit that I hung from my tools to place protection frequently during the early years of my ice climbing career.

## Bad Pro

If the ice is thin, rotten, aerated, or otherwise bad, get creative with your protection. Lacking good screw placements, you may be able to find decent rock pro or natural pro. If not, go for "safety in numbers"—set extra screws hoping that something will catch a fall. Equalizing two or more ice screws increases their holding strength—equalized screws should be 18 inches to 2 feet apart. Clipping dubious ice screws with load-limiting quickdraws (such as Yates Screamers or Charlet Moser Shock Absorbers) can improve their chance of holding a fall (see Chapter 7 for more on load-limiters). Two to four load-limiters on the rack can bolster the first screws in a pitch (those that would take a high-factor lead fall), bad screws up higher, or shaky fixed pro.

A dynamic belay, where the belayer slips a little rope through the belay device when catching the fall, also reduces the force on your lead protection. Climbing with a low-impact rope, equalizing screws, clipping them with a load-limiter, *and* receiving a dynamic belay gives bad pro the best odds of holding. If hard, poorly protected moves exist near the ground, build a pile of snow in the drop zone to create a "bouldering pad." This trick saved me from serious injury once. In the end, though, when facing bad pro, your best survival tactic is to climb in perfect control, or bail before the pro gets bad.

## Thin Ice

The start to *Ames Ice Hose* in southern Colorado is notoriously thin most years. On my first trip up this pitch, I placed three ice

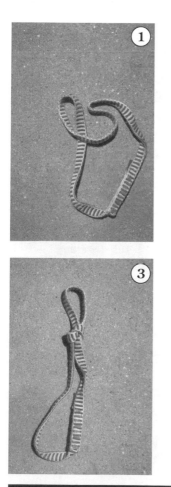

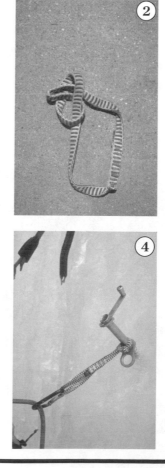

If the ice is so thin that your screw bottoms out before it's fully driven, you may want to tie it off to reduce leverage, especially if it extends more than 2 inches from the ice. Make a slip knot in one of your longer quickdraws. Slip it over the ice screw, slide it down to the ice, and cinch it tightly around the screw. Some climbers carry a handful of slings pre-tied off as in photo 3. Some screws, like this one, have a metal hanger that can slide up and down the screw to reduce leverage. If so, it's better to clip the hanger directly. Note: Tests have shown (at least on Black Diamond ice screws) that it may be better to tie off only screws that protrude more than 2 inches from the ice surface. More on this later.

Probably the strongest way to rig screws in thin ice is shown here. Place 2 screws in a vertical line, 12 or so inches apart. Tie off the lower screw as normal, then support the eye of the lower screw with a cord cinched tight to the upper screw. The cord should be flush with the ice surface on the upper screw, and you can cinch it taut with a trucker's hitch.

A camming, sliding titanium hanger avoids the problems of sling tie-offs.

In thin ice (at least 3 or 4 inches thick) and frozen moss or dirt you can get marginal protection from an ice hook. First, start a nice pick hole with your axe. Set the ice hook in the hole and drive it home with your hammer. It's often a good idea to clip ice hooks to the rope with a load-limiting quickdraw. However, don't expect too much from ice hooks or load-limiters.

hooks. Two of them fell out, so I may as well have soloed the pitch. With no real protection, the key was staying calm, spreading weight between my feet and tools, and only moving on good placements.

Depending on how thin the ice is, protection may or may not be available. For verglas, your best hope is to get rock protection. Or find small clumps of ice that will accept an ice hook or short screw, or some frozen turf, moss, dirt, or crack to drive a hook into.

If patches of ice are at least 4 inches thick, you can set short ice screws, also called stubbies. Carry a good selection of stubbies if you expect much thin ice—a well-placed stubbie is stronger than a longer, tied-off screw. Definitely avoid bulges when setting stubbies—the bulge will plate right off if you fall. Instead, look for flat or slightly concave spots.

If the screw bottoms out on rock with the hanger protruding 2 inches or more from the ice, girth hitch or slip knot a 9/16- or 11/16-inch sling around the shaft, so the anchor gets loaded near the ice to minimize leverage. Otherwise, a fall may bend the screw and pluck it from the ice. A camming metal hanger that locks at the ice surface and can't cut is the best tie-off material. (See Chapter 7 for the lowdown on tie offs.)

Rigging screws in series is probably the strongest way to protect thin ice, though it's rarely done because it's time-consuming and difficult to arrange on steep pitches. But if you need good thin-ice pro, it's a viable technique.

Ice hooks have limited ability to catch a leader fall, though they can protect you through a few moves of sketchy climbing. Ice hooks definitely expand your options for protection. Never place a hook instead of a good screw—they're far less reliable. Ice hooks take practice to place well, and they may tinkle down the rope if not set perfectly. To set an ice hook, make a good starting hole at the same angle as the hook's beak, drive the hook deep, and don't fall! (In qualified defense of the ice hook, Jared Ogden reports a half-placed hook that caught a 20-footer.)

## Natural Protection

Natural protection may be the quickest option, or the only option. Natural pro includes slung pillars, ice bumps, ice tunnels, and trees—creativity is your main limitation. Sometimes you'll chop the ice to open a tunnel or enhance a bollard. The strength of natural ice pro depends on the thickness and quality of the ice—it can be stronger than all but the best of ice screws. Complex natural pro can be slow, so don't get fixated on some fancy natural rig if you can fire in a good screw and move on. Remember, your partner is shivering at the belay.

One option not shown in the photos is to slice a vertical slot in a sheet of ice, or between two pillars, then slip a long screw, or your third tool, through this slot,

*If you can't find a good placement for an ice screw, natural pro may do the trick. Natural protection is often faster (and sometimes more bomber) than placing an ice screw. Tying off the bottom of a stout ice pillar can give good protection, as shown here.*

1. You can get protection by exploiting a natural tunnel in the ice.

2. A small pillar can give some protection, but I wouldn't trust this one too much.

1. Don't expect miracles from a rig like this.

2. You can tie a sling through two or three ice holes and equalize the load on them.

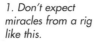

1. On an ice sheet, you can punch two holes through the ice and run a sling through them.

2. On cauliflower ice, you can run a long sling around a giant cauliflower. If you don't have a long sling, chop notches in the cauliflower so it fits the sling you do have, as shown here.

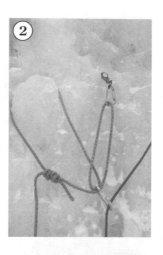

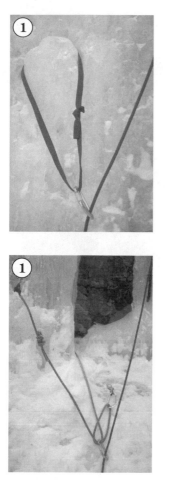

1. You can turn an ice hump into a bollard by chopping a trough for the sling to sit in. Be careful, lest you break the hump off.

2. If your screw is less than bomber, equalizing it to a bollard gives it a better chance of holding. I especially like doing this at the beginning of a pitch if I can't get in a good screw, because the potential force on the first piece of pro is so high.

1. You can also equalize a screw to a small ice pillar. Rigged like this, if the pillar breaks you'll get a lot of extension.

2. If you tie an overhand knot in the cord just above the equalizing point you can minimize the extension if the pillar breaks.

and toggle it sideways. A sling around the middle of the screw or tool gives you something to clip. Tying off the pillars, or threading two holes in the ice sheet—either natural holes or man-made—might be stronger and quicker. A couple of long slings will come in handy. Never pass up the opportunity for easy, natural protection, unless you're certain that good ice for screws exists elsewhere.

## Mixed Pro

Protection on a mixed route can test a climber's creativity and versatility—some routes require cams, nuts, pins, tied-off icicles, and ice screws—but you can find pro if you work at it. Other routes are runout and necky, testing a climber's boldness and technique. A new generation of mixed routes have preplaced bolts or pitons, allowing the climber to focus on the moves, with little danger involved.

Ice anchors are covered thoroughly in the next two chapters. For mixed routes you might add five to eight pins, a set of nuts,

Half ropes work well for ice climbing. By only clipping one strand to each ice screw, you can minimize the force on the piece (by lengthening the stretch in the rope, and hence the distance you fall). Also, if a falling column of ice or errant pick or crampon point hits a rope, you still have another rope. Finally, if you have a wandering pitch, you can route the ropes separately to minimize rope drag. It's good to alternately clip the ropes into your protection unless it's absolutely bomber. If you clip both ropes to the same piece of protection, you increase the force of a lead fall on your protection about 40 percent.

two to four small tri-cams, and a handful of camming units to your ice rack. Rock protection is often easier and quicker to place than ice anchors, and it may be the only choice. Consider clean protection (cams or nuts) first, but you may need pitons. Because you're climbing a waterfall, cracks are often mungy or ice-filled. Try to clear the inside of the crack before setting clean protection, or your piece may not hold. The exception is with pitons, which usually clear their own way into a placement. Angle or Z-pins are often more reliable than blade pins because you get a more biting contact. If you place a pin, you might consider leaving it fixed to avoid the rock damage of pins going in and out with each party. If you find fixed pins, treat them with suspicion, because corrosion and freeze-thaw forces wreak havoc on fixed gear. If you can't get a nut to go in, try pounding it in—good pro gains you a lot of confidence. If you can't get anything bomber, equalizing two or more pieces is often the solution.

See John Long's *Climbing Anchors* and *More Climbing Anchors* (Falcon Publishing) for an exhaustive treatment of rock anchors.

## THE RUN OF THE ROPE

A single rope can work fine on ice, provided you never cut it with your tools, crampons, or a shard of ice or sharp rock. Slippery ice normally negates rope drag, but still, a clever leader keeps the rope running clean through judicious use of quickdraws and slings, taking special care on traverses and roofs. Remember, ropes never break—but they can be cut.

With half ropes, you'll normally clip only one rope into each piece of protection. When single-clipping, designate one rope to run left and one to run right. Clip the ropes alternately, unless you need to clip one rope into successive pieces to keep the ropes running straight. Occasionally, you might clip both ropes into a bomber piece, to avoid relying on one rope. If you have a bad screw, you can set another one nearby and clip one rope into each screw, which somewhat equalizes the pro. Don't confuse half ropes with their skinny cousins twin ropes. Twin ropes must both be clipped into *every* protection piece.

By simplifying the dynamics of climbing ropes, I've estimated that clipping two half ropes generates around 40 percent more impact force on your protection than clipping one. This percentage is subject to error, but the conclusion is clear: it's safer to clip only one rope into sketchy protection. Of course, one rope stretches more than two, increasing your chance of decking on a ledge or the ground.

It sometimes helps to let the belayer know which rope you're clipping. A common signal is to call the rope color—"blue!" means feed blue rope so I can clip. If you've clipped the last piece with the green rope, your belayer can throw slack in blue without increasing your fall if you blow the clip. Calling rope colors is more common in rock climbing, where the clips are often more urgent.

Thoughtful clipping will keep your half ropes running straight. Avoid cross-clipping which creates rope drag, misaligns the direction of pull on the anchor, and worse, could load nylon across nylon and possibly cause rope or quickdraw failure.

## SECONDING A PITCH

The second faces less jeopardy than the leader—the leader and the second may even disagree on a pitch's difficulty, because their experiences were so vastly different. When seconding, usually no penalty exists for falling, unless you're climbing with John Sherman, in which case you have to buy all of his beers that night if you fall where he didn't (quite an expensive proposition). This means you don't always need perfect sticks when seconding. An energy and timesaving tactic for the second is to hook the pick holes left by the leader, and not make every tool placement bomber. This is a great time to practice your hooking. Note: If you are far below the leader, especially if climbing on a skinny rope, a fall might drop you a ways due to rope stretch. In this case, climb carefully and in control.

The major bummer of seconding is cleaning screws. (This inconvenience is more than made up for by the fact that you didn't have to risk your neck on the lead.) To remove a screw, find a restful stance, chop the minimum ice necessary to remove the pro, and screw it out. Clear the ice from the tube before it freezes solid.

## BELAYING

Belaying ice is like belaying rock, except it's colder, and you have to dodge debris knocked off by the leader. Another consideration is the fact that you're often wearing thick gloves or mittens, and this means you have to pay extra attention. Take all the safety precautions—double check tie-in knots, harness buckles, locking carabiners, etc., before climbing.

Always belay far outside the climber's fall line when possible. Belaying beneath an ice climber is like being a clay pigeon in a trap shoot—you're certain to get sprayed with projectiles. And if the leader falls, you might get skewered by various sharp objects! On multi-pitch routes, especially those in a narrow gully, you may be forced to belay in the fall line. Hide under a roof or in a belay cave if possible, or hunker beneath your rucksack. Hope your partner's not a hacker, and never look up.

Bill Alexander looked up one day when he was belaying a long pitch of ice near Cody, Wyoming. As the leader neared the belay, Bill was forced to move closer to the base of the route to give the leader more rope. After the usual barrage of ice stopped (or so he thought), Bill looked up and a large chunk pasted him in the face. He received several facial fractures and required extensive reconstructive surgery. After that, we called him Frankenstein. Dogs barked at him, and women ran away. Don't let this happen to you.

Keep the rope stacked in a tight lap coil, or off to the side, so you don't crampon it or get it caught on icicles below. When belaying a toproped climber, avoid taking rope in when they're swinging a tool—you may pull the rope into the climber's line of fire.

If the leader has bad protection, give him or her a dynamic belay if they fall. Letting a bit of rope out during the catch reduces the impact force on the protection. When wearing big, clumsy gloves or mittens, you can wrap the rope twice around your belay hand to prevent the rope from slipping through your hand in a fall, but then it's hard to give a dynamic belay, and my chiropractor says this is a good way to sprain your hand or wrist.

Plate or tube belay devices work best for belaying on the ice, and they also work well with half ropes and twin ropes. GriGris do not work on iced ropes, and are not well suited to ice climbing. If the ropes become extremely iced, they may jam in your belay device. A figure-8 device might work better on icy ropes, or you may be resigned to a hip belay, which was the standard belay technique before belay devices were popularized in the early 1980s, and is still an important skill to know. To hip belay in the safest manner possible, clip the ropes to your harness, pass them around your back, and clip them to a second carabiner on the other side of your harness. These carabiners prevent the rope from becoming misaligned in a leader fall, so you can make the catch with no problem.

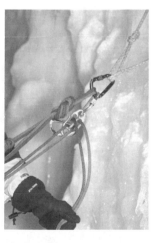

At the belay, if there's no ledge to stack the rope on, you can do a lap coil (stacking the rope back and forth across the rope going from your harness to the anchors), or if you want to keep the rope out of your way, you can stack it on a well-placed ice axe, as shown. Be sure to tie the axe in, so you can't possibly loose it.

The belayer is using a GiGi, popular in Canada and Europe. The GiGi is a self-locking belay device that works great for simultaneously belaying two seconds. The double strands coming out of the top of the GiGi go to the climber(s).

Self-locking belay plates, like the Plaquette and the GiGi, are very popular in Europe, Canada, and in the guiding community, but they haven't yet found widespread use in the United States. They work great for belaying the second directly off the anchors, and if he or she falls, they lock up automatically, with no strength required from the belayer. They're especially useful when climbing with parties of three, though only very experienced climbers should use the system I'm about to describe: The leader arrives at the belay, sets bomber anchors, connects the GiGi directly to the anchors, and rigs both ropes in the device. Now, both seconds follow the pitch simultaneously, climbing two different lines side by side. **It's important that one of the seconds doesn't get too far above the other and shower him or her with ice.** With this technique, parties of three can climb nearly as fast (sometimes faster) than a party of two. Beginning- or intermediate- level climbers should follow one at a time, because you must climb in control to make this system work safely.

## BELAY TRANSITIONS

On long routes, efficiency at the belay transitions makes the climb go faster. Every party finds their own shortcuts and speed tricks. In one system the leader reaches the belay, sets one bomber ice screw, and goes off belay. While the leader finishes arranging the belay anchors, the second cleans all but one good screw from the lower belay. Once the leader has a good belay anchor, he puts the second on belay. At that point, the second removes the final screw and climbs, moving quickly by hooking the leader's old pick holes. At the new belay, the second clips into a sling prearranged by the leader, the team reracks, and the new leader casts off.

Whatever system you work out, keep safety, speed, and efficiency as your priorities. It's good to always ponder, "What could I be doing right now to speed us up?" This doesn't mean giving a sloppy belay while you eat a cheese and salami sandwich. Rather it means not standing around when there are tasks to be done.

## BIG ICE

Before jumping on the megapitch monsters, dial your systems, speed, and efficiency on shorter and medium-length routes. As Jojo says, "first you get good, then you get fast." You'll know when you're ready to up the ante.

Before the big route, research the climbing, route-finding, belays, and descent. Prepare your gear the night before. The lighter you go, the faster you'll climb, but don't leave essential insulation and protection home. When rock climbing, a forced bivi might be uncomfortable and inconvenient; but on an ice route, the unplanned bivi can render you frostbitten and hypothermic. If you choose a route where you descend by rappeling the route, you can easily bail at any time if you're not going fast enough.

*Soloing Bridalveil Falls in Colorado.*
LANE AHERN PHOTO

Start early, and don't waste time on the approach. These days, an early start and fast approach are often necessary to ensure being the first team on the route. Keep a conservative time budget. For example, a team may plan two hours for the approach, half an hour to get ready, one and a half hours per pitch for seven pitches (for a total ten and a half hours of climbing), one hour for the descent, and one hour to ski out. This makes a 15-hour day, so it's obvious you'll want to be climbing by dawn.

Say it's late season, and you have 12 hours of daylight. If you start climbing at daybreak, you'll arrive at the top of the route with one and a half hours of light left. Barring any rappel snafus, you'll be back on the ground with half an hour of light remaining for the ski trip out. In a better world, you climbed faster than the budgeted time, so you have three hours of light left at the top of the route. You can relax somewhat, because now you won't be skiing in the dark.

On the other hand, imagine the route is more desperate than you anticipated, and after eight hours you're only four pitches up. Now you've got four hours of light and three pitches to go. At your current pace, you'll have to climb the last pitch, descend, and ski out in the dark. Better to bail, unless you're prepared and psyched for night climbing.

Short winter days and long cold nights make the ice climber's time budget crucial on long adventures. When you're pushing both ends of the day into darkness, a good headlamp with spare batteries and bulbs is essential gear. Most climbers have an epic story of descending in the dark because they left the lamp at home, or because the batteries or bulb choked at the worst possible moment.

## FREE SOLOING

For a small number of climbers, free soloing is the ultimate expression of climbing. It's also the quickest way to end up in a pine box. Some climbers justify soloing on ice because they can plant their picks as deep as they want, essentially belaying themselves up the route.

One of my best ice climbing days involved soloing Colorado's two megaclassics, *Bridalveil Falls* and *Ames Ice Hose* in southern Colorado. That day was like a dream—the exhilaration and freedom of movement were ethereal. On the other side of the coin, my worst climbing trip ended when I drove home 20 hours alone, after my friend and partner Derek Hersey fell 300 meters free soloing a rock climb in Yosemite.

If you insist on soloing, or making huge runouts for that matter, you'd better be solid and have a good reason for doing it (other than fame, glory, and impressing others). If you blow it, your friends and family are the ones who will suffer.

# Anchors

# CHAPTER 7

*"Clang, clang, clang, whumphff!" I looked down to see a leader whiz 100 feet to the ground, ripping three ice screws like candles from a birthday cake. This man was lucky—he crawled out of the snow and completed his lead.*

## BELAY ANCHORS

The possibilities for rigging belay anchors seem endless. The critical point is to establish a bomber belay, with two or three good, equalized anchors.

When arranging belay anchors, first find a protected location—a belay to the side of the route or under an overhang spares the belayer from being showered by ice. Next, look around and examine the options. Is rock protection available? Where is the ice solid? Plan your setup, then rig it.

Belay and toprope anchors should have at least two bomber screws, placed 18 inches or more apart and equalized. In brittle ice, screws should be 2 to 3 feet apart. If the screws are anything less than bomber, set three; beginners should always set three. You can tie into solidly planted tools to back up the belay anchors. In the best conditions, expect two equalized tools to hold about 2,000 pounds—definitely not enough to serve as your sole belay anchor, but enough to help shore up an already decent anchor arrangement. One system that's good for hanging belays is to equalize two screws, and keep a third screw as a backup, unweighted, so no pressure melting weakens its placement. Triple equalizing three screws probably gives the greatest strength, though.

Here we show many possibilities for rigging a belay, including tying in with a single rope, double ropes, webbing, or a cordelette. How to rig the anchors depends on your gear selection, personal preference, and the given situation.

### One Rope

*Two medium or long ice screws can give an adequate belay, provided both are fully driven in good ice. The leader should set another piece right off the belay. One of the simplest tie-ins is to clove hitch the rope to both screws, and adjust it so the load is somewhat equalized on the screws. It's good to use locking carabiners with clove hitches.*

## One Rope (continued)

*1. The triangle tie-in. If one of the screws is placed off to the side, you can tie into both screws, then clip the rope back to your harness with a clove hitch, so both screws get weighted. The belayer here has also clipped the rope through one of the screws, so if the second falls the belayer will get pulled up rather than down, which is more comfortable and easier to hold.*

*2. A two ice screw belay, backed-up with an ice axe. One of the tie-in knots is a figure-eight, which is the most secure knot, but it's harder to adjust than a clove hitch.*

*1. A two screw belay equalized with a double-length sling. By tying an overhand knot in the long leg of the sling, just above the tie-in point, the belayer has minimized the extension should the top screw blow out.*

*2. The same arrangement as the previous one, only the belayer has backed-up the sling and tie-in carabiner by tying the rope directly to one of the screws. Note the small amount of slack in the rope, so the equalizing point of the sling gets loaded rather than the lower ice screw.*

*1. An equalizing figure-eight allows you to equalize the load on two or three anchors using only the climbing rope. Tie a figure-eight with an extra big loop.*

*2. Now pass that loop back through the top of the figure-eight to create three loops.*

(3)

(4)

3. Clip these loops into your three anchors.

4. If you only have two anchors, collapse one of the loops (important), and clip the two remaining loops into the two anchors. Avoid using the equalizing figure-eight if the anchors are more than a eighteen inches apart, or if they're not bomber, to avoid having the rope run against itself should an anchor pull out. Also, don't use the equalizing figure-8 if the leader is going to need every inch of rope to reach the next belay.

You can also use a cordelette to equalize the load on your anchors. Tie the cordelette into a loop using a double fisherman's knot. Clip the loop into all of the anchors, then pull down a strand of cord between each anchor, in the anticipated direction of loading. Tie the strands together with a figure-8 knot (or an overhand knot if the cord is too short). This knot isolates each loop, so if one loop cuts you don't have total failure. It also prevents extension should one anchor rip. If the direction of pull is different than expected, though, the cordelette will not provide equalization. The beauty of the cordelette is that it creates a single tie-in point, so it's especially efficient if one climber is leading all of the pitches. This is one of the bomber anchors shown here.

Here we have two horizontally-spaced screws, equalized with double slings. The figure-8 tie-in knot is clipped into double carabiners, and the whole thing is backed-up to an ice axe. The belayer has also re-directed the pull by clipping the rope to one of the ice screws. This setup is probably okay, especially given that the ice is fairly soft, but it's generally good to have the screws a little further apart. Some experts claim that ice screws in a belay should be aligned vertically, but in my tests, when an ice screw fails, it blows out of the ice in a semi-circle to the sides and below the screw. In soft ice, the screw hole elongates until the screw bends and breaks or pulls out. So horizontally-spaced screws are okay, provided they're far enough apart. The exception would be if you're anchoring into a small pillar, in which case you should not set the screws at the same horizontal level. The more brittle the ice, the further screws should be apart.

## One Rope (continued)

This belayer has equalized the upper two screws with a doubled cordelette, and clipped into the lowest screw, and the equalized point of the upper screws with clove hitches. Locking carabiners at the tie-in points ensure that the clove hitches can't come untied. Further, the belayer has re-directed the second's rope through one of the high screws. This will be a good point for the climber to hang from when she arrives at the belay and before she casts off on the next lead, because it's off to the side of the belayer's tie-in. With the quickdraw already in place, this screw will also be a good first piece of protection for the next lead. The screw is perfectly placed in a slightly concave section of ice, which makes the placement exceptionally strong.

A direct belay off the anchors. The belayer has equalized two anchors with a piece of cord, and minimized the extension if the top screw fails by tying an overhand knot in the cord. Though it's hard to see, there's a 180-degree twist in one loop of the cord so if one anchor fails, the carabiner doesn't slide off the end of the cord for a total failure.

## Two Ropes

Double ropes give you even more options for rigging the belay. A standard tactic is to clip one of the ropes to a screw, and the other rope to a second screw, as shown here. The belayer has re-directed the rope through the top screw, which can serve as the first piece of protection for the next leader. With only two screws in the belay, though, the leader should place a third screw very early in the pitch.

## Two Ropes (continued)

*1. This belayer has tied one of his half ropes into the lowest ice screw, and the other rope into an equalized point of the upper two screws. The sling equalizing the upper two screws is tied off to eliminate extension if one of the screws fails. The belayer has also re-directed the belay rope through one of the high ice screws. A nice bomber arrangement.*

*1. Another effective belay is to tie each half rope into a separate screw, then run the belay rope through a third, higher screw. The upper screw must be solid or you risk dropping the second a ways if he falls. This arrangement gives the second a good place to clip in when he arrives at the belay. This is my favorite setup if I doubt my partner's ability or willingness to set a good screw right above the belay as he leads past.*

*2. Not smart. This climber is risking his life and his partner's by belaying off of two ice axes. This may be okay in an emergency situation, but only if both axes are sunk to the hilt, the climber being belayed is seconding, and the belayer has a really good stance. It's definitely not safe to lead above this belay. It figures that he's not even wearing a helmet.*

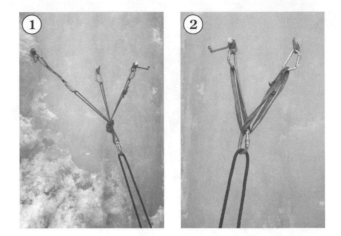

1. For toproping,
three ice screws
rigged with a
cordelette give a
bomber anchor. Tie
the cordelette off to
eliminate extension if
a screw fails, and to
make each leg of the
cordelette
independent. Double
carabiners where the
rope runs provide
complete redundancy.

2. Two equalized
bombproof screws
can make a good
toprope anchor,
provided they're not
exposed to the sun,
and the air
temperature is below
freezing. Double
slings and carabiners
provide redundancy.
Whether you have
two screws or three,
check your toprope
anchors periodically
to make sure the
screws are not
melting out from
pressure, meltwater,
or sunshine.

All these anchors look and sound good in the book. In reality,
sometimes you can't find good anchors. In this case, climb
higher and try another spot. If you absolutely can't get bomber
anchors, set at least three ice screws, equalize them, and back up
the belay with your ice tools. Make sure you have a good stance,
belay off your harness, and if the second falls, hold the weight on
your harness rather than loading the marginal anchors. The
leader of the next pitch should place good gear as soon as
possible.

## FALL FACTOR

The fall factor is an important but largely unknown or misunder-
stood concept. It's pretty simple, really. The fall factor is the
distance you fall divided by the amount of rope out. The greater
the fall factor, the greater the force on your protection.

Say you're 10 feet above the belay on a vertical pitch with no
protection in. If you fall, you'll drop 20 feet before the rope starts
to stretch, which gives you a fall factor of 20/10 = 2. This is the
maximum fall factor. The fall factor, rope, and weight of the
climber determine the impact force on your protection. A 20-foot,
factor 2 fall theoretically creates the same force as a 100-foot
factor 2 fall. Even though the second fall is longer, more rope is
out to absorb the energy of the fall.

It's hard to say exactly what this force will be. In its rope tests,
the UIAA drops a 176-pound weight 16.4 feet(5 meters) onto 9.2
feet(2.8 meters) of rope, to create a severe factor 1.78 fall. The
UIAA specifies that a rope must limit the force on the climber to
2,640 pounds or less in its first drop test. Many ropes test well
below this. With 2,640 pounds on the climber, we assume the force
on the belayer will be about 60 percent of that, as reported by REI.
If we ignore rope drag, the top piece must hold the combined force
on the climber and the belayer, or 1.6 times the force on the
climber. Thus, in the UIAA fall, using the least dynamic rope
allowed, the top piece could get hit with 4,224 pounds. This is
more than the strength of most climbing protection, and near the

strength of carabiners. The impact force increases or decreases roughly proportionate with the weight of the climber. So if you weigh 200 pounds when you're decked out in ice gear and clothing, a high impact rope in a high factor fall could load your top anchor up to 4,800 pounds, definitely enough to blow out carabiners and all but the best constructed and placed ice screws. A light climber, weighing only 140 pounds with gear, might put only 3,360 pounds on the top anchor in the same fall with the same rope, which is definitely a significant reduction in force. From what I've seen, however, many ice climbers fall into the burly category. Fortunately, many ropes are well below the UIAA limits in impact force, because they stretch a lot.

## ICE PROTECTION: HOW STRONG IS IT?

Stories abound of ice screws holding amazing leader falls. Other tales speak of ice screws ripping out, carabiners breaking, and the unlucky leader hitting the deck. What can you expect from your ice climbing protection?

In 1997, we spent many days testing ice protection in Ouray and Boulder Canyon, Colorado, trying to answer this question. We broke ice screws, pound-ins, hooks, threads, and axes by pulling them with a come-along, and hurling a 185-pound test weight off a waterfall. The verdict: good ice is really good, and bad ice is really bad. The strength of ice varies incredibly,

Ice screw testing under the bridge in Ouray, Colorado. Cranking up the load with a five-ton come-along, and measuring the force with a 20,000-pound dynamometer.

The carnage.

depending on its temperature, density, thickness, geometry and crystal structure.

Obviously, ice protection is only as strong as the surrounding ice. We saw ice screws fail as low as 300 pounds, as high as 7,000 pounds, and everywhere in between. Ice must be dense and homogeneously frozen to provide good holding strength. Air pockets or liquid water create voids in the ice structure, weakening the ice. Geometry is critical too. Screws placed in a solid, flat, or concave section of good ice are almost always bomber, but those set above a bulge, on a narrow column, or in aerated or chandelier ice are often frighteningly weak.

## Drop Tests

Chris Harmston, quality assurance manager for Black Diamond, and I performed drop tests at the Ouray Ice Park, where the manmade ice is often aerated—not the best ice for protection. The air temperature ranged from 10 degrees F to 28 degrees F. To conduct the tests, a 16.4-foot(5-meter) section of 10.5-mm dynamic lead rope was clipped to an equalized anchor, and the other end was weighted with 185 pounds of iron. The iron test weight was raised to the end of the rope, and the rope was clipped through protection. Then we dropped the test weight.

The results were dramatic: In drops of 16 to 28 feet, with corresponding fall factors of 1 to 1.7, the top screw ripped out in 7 out of 12 tests, and carabiners broke three times. Ice hooks failed three times in three tests. In the most sobering test, the test mass dropped 16 feet (factor 1 fall) onto a chrome-moly pound-in clipped with a Screamer. This was the fourth drop on the test rope (with one hour between drops), so the rope's elasticity was compromised. First, the Screamer's stitches blew out, then the clipping carabiner broke. The test weight fell 5 more feet onto two equalized screws, where the hanger broke off of one screw, and the locking carabiner at the equalized point broke. Ouray guide Mike O'Donnell and I observed this test from across the gorge. We looked at each other, big-eyed, and vowed to quit ice climbing.

One year after these tests, a climber in Vail replicated this drop test. He fell, ripped out an ice hook, then an ice screw, and finally broke a carabiner, landing on the ground.

In real climbing situations, locking carabiners almost never break, so it's obvious that the drop tests were unrealistically severe. What the tests point out is that climbing gear doesn't have much safety margin in worst-case falls. Weight and size limitations and market demands have equipment designers building gear that is just strong enough for the duty. Therefore, climbers need to be prudent with their protection, especially when close to the belay, where a high factor fall is possible and few backup anchors are in place.

In the drop tests, the belay and test masses were both static, resulting in an overly severe fall. In a real climbing situation the belayer would be lifted slightly, a little rope might slip through the belay device, and the leader's body, being somewhat elastic, would decelerate slower than an iron test mass. These factors create a more dynamic belay, and decrease the impact force. Without dynamics in the belay, for example if the belayer is tied in very tight to the anchors and belaying with a self-locking belay device, the impact force on your protection can become dangerously high, especially if you're corn-fed, close to the belay, and climbing on an abused rope.

To make the drop test more realistic, we rigged the belay rope through an ATC belay device at the anchors, and back-weighted the rope with 75 pounds to simulate a strong brake hand. (A typical climber would more likely hold 30 to 50 pounds with the brake hand.) We also decreased the fall factor. With this "dynamic" belay, ice screws held three out of three falls, with fall factors between 0.9 and 1.2, and a threaded tunnel held a 0.8 fall factor drop. Ice hooks went zero for three, failing even when clipped with a load-limiting quickdraw, which blew all of its stitches. Unfortunately, we conducted only a handful of tests with the dynamic belay. These tests reaffirmed my faith in good protection and the belay system, but not in ice hooks.

Load-limiting quickdraws can help decrease the force of a fall, but most of what has been written about them is erroneous. One ice climbing book claims they limit the load to 700 pounds, where another ice book and magazine gear review report that they "absorb 500 pounds of impact." The truth is, the load-limiters currently available have a limited capacity to absorb the energy of a long leader fall. A Yates Screamer, for example, can absorb around 500 foot-pounds of energy before all the stitches rip out (according to John Yates, who manufactures and sells them).

Let's say that a climber weighs 170 pounds (decked out in ice gear). After falling 3 feet, he has developed about 510 foot-pounds of kinetic energy (170 pounds x 3 feet = 510 foot-pounds). If an ice screw clipped with a load-limiter catches the climber after a 3-foot fall, the stitches will all rip out, but the load-limiter will do its job, limiting the force on the protection to the activation force—around 550 pounds for a Yates Screamer.

More typically, an ice climber falls further than 3 feet. If the same leader plummets 30 feet, he will develop 5,100 foot-pounds of kinetic energy (30 feet x 170 pounds). The load-limiter has the capacity to absorb only 500 foot-pounds of energy, or about 10 percent of the kinetic energy developed in the fall. This 10 percent may help your gear hold, but the load-limiter contributes less force reduction than we've been promised. According to this simple theoretical analysis, the load-limiter makes any fall seem 3 feet shorter to the protection, for a 170-pound climber. If the climber (with gear) weighs 200 pounds, the load-limiter will absorb the energy developed in 2.5 feet of falling, so falls will seem 2.5 feet shorter to the protection; likewise, a 140-pound climber gets her falls reduced by 3.5 feet.

The results predicted by this theoretical analysis appeared to be somewhat true in the drop tests. The load-limiters would quickly rip through all of their stitches, then the force would spike well above the

*A load-limiting quickdraw.*

activation force of the load-limiter, and the protection would rip out.

In actual falls on a climbing wall conducted 18 months later, Screamers fortunately helped reduce the force more than predicted by this theoretical conjecture. When clipped to the top anchor with a standard quickdraw, 20-foot falls with 20 feet of rope out (factor 1) developed between 1,800 and 2,500 pounds on the top anchor, with my body weight of 165 pounds. The lower forces occurred when my belayer was unanchored, and lifted off the ground during the fall. The higher forces occurred when the belayer was anchored to the ground, demonstrating the value of a dynamic belay. Clipped with a Yates Screamer, however, the same falls produced 1,000 to 1,200 pounds of force, a significant reduction in force that could save you if you fall onto ice protection. Still, falls as short as 5 feet ripped all the stitches out of a Screamer.

Dan Osman, who weighs about 160 pounds, jumped 165 feet on a free-hanging 165-foot rope, and developed around 2,500 pounds of force, showing that a factor 1 fall of 165 feet truly generates about as much force as a factor 1 fall of 20 feet. Unfortunately the force reduction afforded by a Screamer in these huge falls was not measured, but I would expect the force to go over 2,000 pounds in a fall of this length, even with a Screamer. With luck, you'll never fall *that* far.

### Static Tests

The static tests confirmed that ice protection is strong in good ice. Cranking with a come-along while measuring force with a dynamometer, I tested screw placements in Ouray's aerated ice, with air temperatures between 8 degrees F and 32 degrees F, and in Boulder Canyon, where the ice was solid green in the morning, and wet in the afternoon, and temperatures spanned 20 degrees F to 42 degrees F.

Given the variability of the ice, and the limited number of screws for testing, many of the conclusions presented here are not proven with statistical validity, but they are substantiated by results from Black Diamond's testing labs, and REI field testing.

### How Ice Screws Fail

We observed several types of failure in the static tests, and learned about the limitations of ice protection. Foremost: don't expect miracles. Pro in terrible ice is terrible pro, as evidenced by the handful of screws that failed below 1,000 pounds. Many of these were in ice so aerated that the threads were not biting. Ice failure caused nearly one-fourth of the screws and pound-ins to pull below 2,000 pounds, which is less than the force generated in a hard leader fall. Most were set in aerated or slushy ice, on an ice bulge, or not fully driven and not tied off.

One-fourth of the screws held between 2,000 and 3,000 pounds, sufficient to stop most falls on ice. Half of the screws held 3,000 or more pounds, roughly the strength of most spring-loaded camming devices. The failures above 2,000 pounds occurred many different ways. Often, cold, brittle ice would shatter; warm ice would deform and the screw hole would elongate; and bulgy or convex ice would dinner plate. When the supporting ice at the surface failed, short screws (4 inches long) would pull out of the ice. Medium and long screws (6 to 8 inches) would bend, then pull out or break, or the hanger would pull off. For a screw to reach its full strength potential, the ice must fully support the screw.

When the supporting ice did not fail, all models of screws consistently held over 3,000 pounds, and failure was due to the hanger, quickdraw, or carabiner breaking. Most of the time I could predict the weak placements, but more than once I was surprised when a seemingly good screw tested poorly. The strength distribution of the ice pro placements closely follows the trends exhibited in Black Diamond's lab tests, only their lab-prepared test ice typically gave 1,000 to 1,500 pounds more strength compared to the real ice I tested. If these field tests had been restricted to solid, dense ice, the results might be more on par with Black Diamond's lab tests.

In fortyone tests, the average strength of medium and long screws (not tied off) was 3,300 pounds. Carabiners often failed in the tests above 4,000 pounds, though twice they broke at 2,600 pounds, well below their rated strength. The ice may have pushed the carabiner gates open, or off-axis loading may have occurred, undermining the strength of these carabiners.

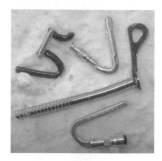

*Three carabiners broke—at 4,200, 5,000, and 6,200 pounds—while this 22-centimeter chrome-moly screw held strong.*

*A screw placed in good ice can be stronger than the carabiner connecting it to the rope.*

*A screw placed in bad ice might barely hold body weight. This 10-centimeter screw broke out of the ice at 300 pounds. Actually, the ice wasn't that bad, but the screw was placed in an ice bulge. When the outer 3 inches of the bulge fractured, the short screw wasn't deep enough to keep holding. Short screws can be strong, however, when placed in a flat or slightly concave section of good ice. Half of the short screws tested to 3,000 pounds or above.*

*An aluminum screw placed in an ice bulge. The bulge fractured at 1,500 pounds, and the screw pulled out. The screw was undamaged.*

1. A 17-centimeter chrome-moly ice screw placed in semi-soft ice.

2. At 1,600 pounds, the hole has elongated substantially, and the screw is starting to bend.

3. At 4,000 pounds, the screw had buckled, and pulled out a couple of inches.

4. At 4,100 pounds, the screw pulled out of the ice. This is plenty strong enough to catch most falls.

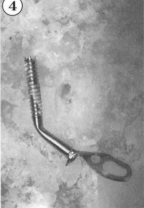

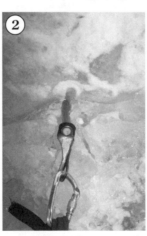

1. This 22-centimeter chrome-moly screw was placed in an ice bulge. At 800 pounds, the surface ice broke, leaving the outer 3 inches of the screw unsupported.

2. At 1,500 pounds, the screw is starting to bend.

3. At 2,000 pounds, the screw has bent more, and is beginning to pull out. This screw finally broke mid-shaft at 2,400 pounds.

A small diameter screw isn't as stiff as a larger diameter one, so it bends more easily, placing greater force on the surface ice. At 2,600 pounds, this titanium screw in soft ice has bent almost 90 degrees, and the screw hole is elongated.

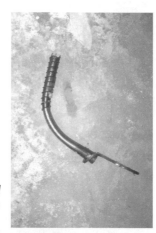

The screw pulled out at 2,700 pounds, enough to catch some falls, but not a substantial fall close to the belay.

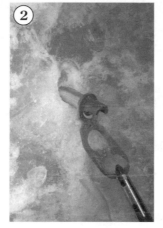

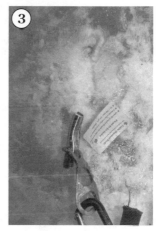

1. A titanium pound-in. At 2,000 pounds the screw hole has elongated, and the pound-in is starting to bend.

2. At 2,600 pounds, the pound-in is bending more, and starting to pull out.

3. This pound in broke at 2,850 pounds.

Not all titanium screws are weak. It depends on the design and the manufacturer. This screw reached 3,700 pounds before the hanger broke.

During the tests, two carabiners failed well below their stated strengths. This one broke at 2,600 pounds, presumably because the gate was pushed open by an ice bulge. Be careful that the ice where your carabiner lies is flat.

## Size Matters

Stubbies, the 4-inch-long wonder screws (I wonder if it's going to hold?) have their place: in thin ice, and never as a substitute for longer screws when climbing thick ice. In 17 tests, stubbies held 300 to 4,100 pounds, with an average strength of 2,670 pounds. In good ice, stubbies often held over 3,000 pounds, but they were less predictable than longer screws. The real beauty of stubbies is that they rarely break, they just pull out, so you can use 'em again after you get out of the hospital.

Medium length screws (6 to 7 inches) held strong in good ice. A 6-inch Black Diamond chrome-moly screw was strongest in the test, reaching 7,000 pounds. We didn't test enough long screws to compare them with medium-length screws. We did learn that even the longest screws are weak in bad ice: one long screw pulled out of terrible ice at 500 pounds. A disproportionate number of the long screws were tested in poor ice, so the results are skewed.

In tests conducted by REI engineers in glacial ice, long screws were substantially stronger than medium-length screws of the same brand. Diameter also appeared to be important in the glacial ice. Fat, 22.5-millimeter-diameter x 18-centimeter-long aluminum screws slightly outperformed all others tested, even the longer 17-millimeter x 22-centimeter screws. In Black Diamond's lab-prepared ice, length had less influence on strength.

## To Tie Off, or Not to Tie Off

It's best to fully drive your screws or pound-ins, and clip the hanger directly with a quickdraw. With the screw less than fully driven, leverage undermines its strength. The tests clearly demonstrated the obvious: the more extended the ice screw, the weaker the placement. With screws 4 inches extended and not tied off, the highest breaking strength in two tests was a pathetic 1,100 pounds. In six tests of Black Diamond 22-centimeter screws, with 2 to 3 inches of leverage on the screw, and no tie off, strengths ranged from 1,400 to 4,200 pounds, with the average being 2,750 pounds. Black Diamond's lab tests showed a similar drop-off in strength for screws not fully driven, with the overall strengths 500 to 1,000 pounds higher in the lab-prepared ice.

Many climbers carry their screws tied off with nylon or Spectra webbing. Once the screw is halfway placed, they can clip, relax, and finish setting the screw. If the screw is not fully driven, either because the ice is thin or the leader is lazy, a tie off is already in place to reduce leverage on the screw. For desperate placements, it may pay to carry a couple of pre-tied-off screws, so you can clip the screw as soon as you get it started. After fully driving the screw, however, clip in with a quickdraw, and unclip the prerigged draw, because in the tests, tied offs were not impressive.

To tie off or not to tie off? The result would have probably been the same for this 22-centimeter chrome-moly screw. At 1,500 pounds, the screw started to bend.

At 2,000 pounds, the sling slipped up to the hanger. At this point, you may as well be clipped to the hanger, because the tie-off sling is no longer reducing leverage. Rather, it has become the weak link. This screw broke at 2,100 pounds, but it had been previously abused in another test, which points out that after you take a hard fall onto a screw, you should retire it. Usually during testing, tie-off slings would cut on the hanger.

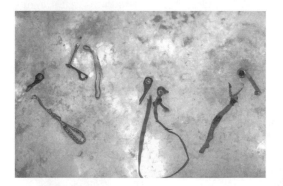

These slings were cut on the hanger during the tests. Typically, the slings would slide out to the hanger around 2,000 pounds due to surface ice failure and bending of the screw. Then the screw would bend further, and the tie off would cut on the hanger at between 2,000 and 3,400 pounds. The broken screw is the one from the previous photo.

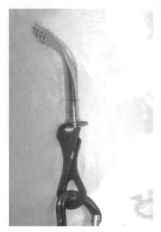

This 22-centimeter screw was placed with the hanger extended 1 inch from the ice, and the hanger was clipped directly. At 1,000 pounds the ice supporting the screw shattered, leaving the hanger extended 2 inches from the surface of the ice. At 1,500 pounds, the screw is starting to bend.

At 4,000 pounds, the ice shattered again, and the screw bent severely and started to pull out. The load dropped to 1,000 pounds, because tension from the come-along decreased after the screw bent.

After re-loading the bent screw to 1,900 pounds, the hanger broke off.

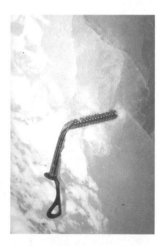

The hanger was clipped directly on this 22-centimeter screw placed with 3 inches of extension. The screw started bending at 800 pounds. Here, the screw is bending further at 1,000 pounds.

Impressively, this screw continued holding until the ice shattered at 3,200 pounds, even though it was severely bent.

As the load was increased during the tests, ice screws would bend when the supporting surface ice failed, and the tie-off sling would slide up to the hanger. Then the screw would break or pull out, or the sling would cut on the hanger. In ten tests with tied-off screws, with the screws 0 to 2.5 inches from fully driven, the strength ranged from 2,000 to 3,400 pounds. Nylon tie-off slings were the weakest. The average strength with tie offs was 2,530 pounds, slightly less than stubbies, and even less than screws 2 to 3 inches extended and not tied off. The conclusion: a tie-off sling definitely weakens a screw fully driven in good ice. A tie off may or may not strengthen a screw placed with a couple of inches of leverage. Personally, if the screw is angling down, with 2 inches or less of leverage, I'll clip the hanger directly. If it's angling up, especially with 2 inches or more of leverage, I'll tie it off with a Spectra sling. One smaller problem with pre-tying off screws is that when the webbing on the screw becomes wet and freezes, the screw becomes harder to place and rack.

## What Angle?

For years we've been taught to set ice screws 15 to 20 degrees above the line perpendicular to the ice (with the hanger above the threads) so they hold like a tent peg or a hook. Setting the tube at this angle is akin to bending a stick across your knee to break it—it places higher stress on the surface ice, and greater bending stress on the screw, so the ice shatters and the screw bends and breaks more easily. Our tests, Black Diamond's tests, and REI's tests suggest that, in good ice, screws with ample threads hold better when set at 15 to 20 degrees below the perpendicular line. Our tests even showed good strength with screws placed 40 degrees below perpendicular, though REI's glacial ice tests gave a weak result for a pound-in placed at 45 degrees down, which you would expect because of the minimal thread surface area. The spiral length of the threads on most screws gives 1.5 to 2.5 square inches of thread surface area, so screws hold amazingly well against the outward pull when angled below the perpendicular line—if the ice is good. Based on

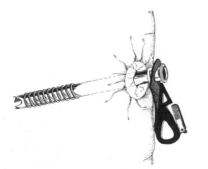

Screws placed at this angle in good ice shatter the surface ice and bend or break at less than full strength.

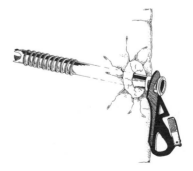

In good ice, screws angled down like this give the highest strength, provided that the ice is good and the screw has aggressive threads and a well-designed hanger.

these tests, I recommend setting ice screws and pound-ins 15 to 20 degrees below the perpendicular line, if the ice is solid and the screw has ample threads.

If the ice is not solid, some climbers advise returning to the upward lean with your screws. The truth is, not enough testing has been done to predict the best angle in this case, and each placement is unique. Finding the optimal angle in bad ice may be a moot point, because if the teeth aren't biting well, the placement is worthless regardless of the placement angle. Manufacturers could improve the strength of their screws in marginal ice by running threads the full length of the screw.

**There are three important exceptions to this rule of angling your screws down:** (1) if "melt-out" conditions exist, either due to sunshine, warm temperatures, or flowing water, because these conditions undermine the pullout strength of the screw; (2) if the screw or pound-in does not have aggressive threads for holding outward pull, which includes all pound-ins; (3) or if the hanger is poorly designed to handle an outward pull, usually because it is held in place by a narrow lip on the end of the screw.

### Material

Ice screws are made from chrome-moly, titanium, or aluminum. Screws made from all three materials are strong enough to catch your fall if placed in good ice. The chrome-moly and large-diameter aluminum and titanium tubes are quite stiff, so they crush the surface ice less, and hence tested stronger than the skinny titanium screws (16-millimeter-diameter or less) which bend more easily. More chrome-moly screws would have held loads over 5,000 pounds in the tests, but the carabiners broke rather than the screw or the ice.

Although small-diameter titanium screws are slightly weaker in the ice, they're also light and cheap. If you carry skinny titanium screws, use the stronger, heavier, chrome-moly screws at the belay and early in the pitch, when potential forces are high. Save the lighter, weaker screws for way up on the pitch when the force of a lead fall is relatively low.

### Brand

The quality of ice is far more important than the brand of screw. Every model of screw held at least 2,800 pounds in good ice, and every model pulled out under ridiculously low loads in bad ice. One of the most important considerations is having screws that place easily, so you're likely to deploy them more often.

Once you find a brand that you like, buy a bunch and stick with them. The British Changabang North Face expedition saved weight by carrying half a dozen lightweight, cheap, titanium screws, rather than durable, but heavier, chrome-moly screws. By the time they were halfway up the route, all the screws they hadn't dropped were hopelessly dull or useless, making the climbing much slower, dangerous, and scary. Sadly, one of the team members was swept to his death by an avalanche while establishing a rappel station, unanchored.

## When to Retire Screws

I usually retire my ice screws when I lose them. Otherwise, I use them as long as they are easy to place. Once the threads and teeth get dinged up and it's a liability trying to set the screw, I ditch it as a rappel anchor, or give it away to my enemies.

One screw in the tests appeared undamaged after breaking through the ice at 4,000 pounds. In a later test, the hanger broke at 1,500 pounds. If you take a hard fall onto a screw or pound-in, it may be structurally damaged without showing visible evidence. Best to chuck it.

## Captain Hook

Some climbers say ice hooks have revolutionized thin and mixed climbing. (Note: they don't work in ultra-thin ice, but if you get 3 or 4 inches of thickness, you can plant a hook). We found that even the best hook placements in ice are sketchy for high-force falls, but they will hold body weight, and might hold a short fall. Ice hooks usually failed by levering and shearing out of the ice. A hook with a longer stem than currently available would limit

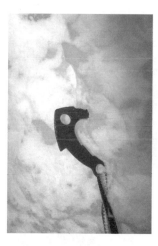

The ice hooks available as this book went to press were not impressive during testing. Because the stem is so short relative to the hook, they have a tendency to lever out when loaded. This chrome-moly hook was initially fully driven. At 400 pounds, it's beginning to lever out. This one pulled out at a mere 600 pounds, though several tested to around 1,600 pounds.

Now you see it.

Now you don't. These titanium hooks averaged around 1,100 pounds.

levering, and increase the strength and reliability of a hook placement. We did not test ice hooks pounded into icy cracks.

The tiniest hooks would be good for aid climbing and pounding into icy cracks, but not much more. In 12 tests, they ranged from 200 to 950 pounds, with an average strength of 600 pounds. Ushba's titanium hooks were substantially stronger. In five tests, they ranged from 800 to 1,400 pounds, with the average being 1,140 pounds. Black Diamond's Spectres were consistently the strongest ice hooks, ranging from 600 to 1,750 pounds, with the average strength in 12 tests being 1,400 pounds. It doesn't take much of a lead fall to generate 1,400 pounds, and I shudder to think of the times I was sketching above an ice hook, but didn't fall.

### Ice Axes

Many ice climbers incorporate their ice axes into the belay, and some have even left a tool in the pitch for protection. The axes I tested were not good samples. Two had been recalled for weak shafts, and one was trashed from two seasons in Patagonia. Nonetheless, the tools were disappointingly weak. Two tools broke at the shaft, and the bolt holding the pick on the other tool sheared, all at around 1,100 to 1,200 pounds. If you do incorporate your axes into the belay, equalize them, and rig so they only get loaded if the ice screws fail, to prevent damaging your axes.

### Natural Pro

The ice we tested was not good for natural protection. It would be possible to get stronger results in better ice. Still, all the Abalakov threads (covered in Chapter 8) we tested (except one,

The shaft of this axe broke at 1,200 pounds.

The screws fastening the pick on this axe sheared at 1,200 pounds. An ice axe does not make a good belay.

This Abalakov thread impressively held 1,550 pounds in bad ice. Other threads broke as low as 800 pounds, and as high as 2,700 pounds.

which was obviously in terrible ice) were strong enough to serve as a rappel anchor. Bollards tested weaker. Make sure the ice is sturdy if you're using a bollard.

## SUMMARY AND CONCLUSIONS

- The most important skill in setting ice pro is the ability to judge the ice, and find the best places to set gear.
- The only sure bet for bomber pro is a flat or concave section of solid blue, green, or yellow ice.
- Screws should be angled 15 to 20 degrees below perpendicular to the surface of the ice, if the ice is solid, the screw has high-relief threads, and melting-out is not likely to occur.
- Fully drive your screws whenever possible.
- Scrutinize the placement as the screw goes in. Feel the turning resistance all the way in. If the screw suddenly turns very easily, you've hit an air pocket. If you don't feel solid ice again within a couple of turns, find a better placement.
- "One-stick" ice is fun and easy to climb, but it may bode poorly for protection because air or liquid water exists in the ice. Try hard to find more solid ice for your screws and pound-ins.
- Don't trust screws set in bad ice.
- Avoid setting pro in or near bulges or on small columns.
- Always clear weak or brittle surface ice before setting protection.
- Clear ice below the screw so the carabiner won't be loaded over an edge, or have its gate pushed open.
- Use carabiners and slings that are in good condition, because you're often counting a lot on each placement.
- Sharp edges on the hanger of some screws (and bolt hangers) can cut dangerous notches into carabiners. Avoid these, or inspect and replace your carabiners as needed.
- Long- and medium-length screws are often stronger and more predictable than short ones, especially if the ice is bulgy, aerated, or wet.
- Place long screws at belays and early in the pitch, when the force of a fall is high.
- If you've already fallen onto a piece of ice pro, don't trust the placement to catch a second fall. If you do, inspect the protection and the surrounding ice first.
- Retire any screw and carabiner that's held a hard, high-factor fall.
- Tie-off slings on fully driven screws are a bad idea.
- Spectra beats nylon for tie-off slings because it's stronger and more resistant to cutting.
- The threads of your screw must bite the ice well for a placement to be strong.
- Air pockets in the ice are bad for your protection.
- Ice hooks are sketchy.
- Small-diameter, high-elongation ropes are good for ice climbing, because they decrease the force on your gear.

- Load-limiting quickdraws (such as Screamers) have limited ability to absorb the energy of a fall. Don't count on them to make bad pro good. They might help.
- Large climbers should pay extra care to have bomber protection.
- Never take shortcuts on your belay anchors.
- Ice axes can supplement, but should not replace ice screws in the belay.
- The leader should set good protection just above the belay, clip it and climb on, then set a second piece shortly thereafter to control the fall factor.
- Climb in control, and avoid falling. Lead as if you're soloing.
- It all comes down to experience, knowing whether your pro is good or not. If the pro is not good, and you can't get anything better, you need to step up to the plate with technique and confidence, or bail.

# Gettin' Down

*"What goes up, must come down."*

Once you're up, how do you get down? Depending on the situation, you'll walk off, downclimb, rappel, or lower. The tools and techniques for descending are fairly straightforward, but a mistake can cost you your life. Descents range from a simple rappel off a tree, to a complicated, devious, and dangerous descent down a mountain face. Good judgement, attention to details, awareness of hazards, and religious double-checking will help keep you alive.

Always have a plan for the descent before going up a route. Epics have been suffered because a party neglected to research the descent. Many guidebooks include information on descending a route. Other climbers may also provide descent beta. If you can't find descent information, scope the route from the ground. Look for places to walk or climb down; if you find none, look for established rappel anchors. If you can't find an obvious descent, rappel the route you climbed, to avoid descending irreversibly into unknown terrain.

Walking down should be the first option, provided the walk-off is easy and not avalanche prone. If the downclimb is technical, or if avalanche conditions exist, though, it's usually safer and more convenient to rappel.

## Downclimbing

Many descents require a bit of downclimbing. If you haven't made the descent before you probably have little knowledge of the terrain below, so be cautious. If you've scoped the descent from the ground, you'll have an idea where to go. Don't be afraid to pull out the rope and rappel or belay if things get hairy—never down-solo anything you don't feel totally confident about. Likewise, never coerce your partners to down-solo anything they aren't comfortable with. Instead, be the first to offer a rope. When downclimbing, stay close together so both climbers have ready assistance, and so the team doesn't get separated.

If you're the stronger partner, go down first to find the logical route, though another option is to lower your partner, or have them rappel, then downclimb to them. Or send the weaker climber down first with a toprope, placing protection for the stronger partner to "down-lead" (hopefully the "weaker" partner knows how to place good protection). Rappeling is usually safer and quicker than down-leading, though, provided you find good rappel anchors.

For leaders, downclimbing is an essential skill. Imagine you're 15 feet above a sketchy piece, and 25 feet above the next one. The route doesn't go, and you can't find good protection to bail from. The sane leader has one option—*downclimb*.

Rappeling from double Abalakov anchors on *The Replicant, Canadian Rockies*, with *The Terminator* in the background and *Sea of Vapors* in the foreground.

It's a good idea to practice downclimbing on toprope before you do much leading. On low-angled downclimbs, face out to see where you're going. As the angle steepens, turn sideways. Steeper still, turn and face the ice.

Keep something in reserve on serious (i.e. runout) leads, so you have the strength to downclimb if you get in a bind. If you're totally pumped, you can hang on your tools to recover some strength before climbing back down.

## Rappeling

Often, rappeling finishes a long, hard day, or comes in the face of miserable weather, when you might be less focused. Keep that guard up until the end, because you're not done until you're cuddled up next to your honey, smugly dreaming about your wild adventures.

If the rappel anchors are fixed, inspect them, and if there's any doubt, give them a bounce test while each member of the climbing party is still tied into solid backup anchors. The anchors must be strong, and the slings or cord in good condition. If they're less than bomber, back them up if possible, and equalize everything. **Don't fall into the sloppy habit of mindlessly trusting fixed gear.**

Short climbs often have trees at the top to rappel from—where there's water, trees will follow, unless you're above timberline. If you anchor off a tree, make sure it's solid. Two ice climbers in Valdez experienced a fatal surprise when a traditional rappel tree uprooted, dumping both of them 200 feet to the ground. To prevent damaging the tree, or sticking your rope, pass the rope through a sling rather than directly around the tree. Add rappel rings to the slings for popular rappels. Also, avoid cramponing the roots of the tree, or you'll be killing your belay anchor.

Long routes may require several rappels. You'd prefer not to leave your 50-dollar ice screws—fortunately better alternatives exist. If you're lucky, the rappel anchors are fixed. If they are fixed, be sure to check that the webbing or cord is in good condition, and that the anchors are bombproof. If the rappel anchors are not fixed, rock anchors or old "leaver" screws might do the trick. You might anchor the rope around a big icicle or through two holes in the ice. The holes might be natural, or you can make them by punching into an air pocket.

Many climbers' favorite trick is to make a V-thread in the ice—also called an Abalakov thread, after the early Russian mountaineer who invented the technique, and the first rock-camming devices. Abalakovs are widely used in the Canadian Rockies, where the long climbs and complex terrain often dictate rappeling the route. To create an Abalakov thread, make two intersecting ice screw holes, and thread them with a 4-foot section of cord or webbing. It helps to have a threading tool, such as a cable with a sharp hook on the end, to pull the cord through the holes. In lieu of this specialized tool, a piece of coat hanger with the end bent into a hook can work, and so can the

1. An Abalakov thread. Make the first hole by setting a long screw to full depth, angled about 60 degrees sideways to the ice surface, then back the screw halfway out.

2. Using the first screw for alignment, set a second screw 6 to 8 inches to the side of the first, angled 60 degrees from the ice surface, toward the first screw hole. You can ensure intersection of the screw holes by viewing both screws from the side, to make sure the second one lines perfectly up with the first. Once the screw holes intersect, back both screws out.

3 and 4. Thread your cord or webbing into one hole, grab it with a hooked piece of coat wire, and pull it out the second hole. You'll need 3.5 or 4 feet of 6- to 8-millimeter cord, or 9/16- to 1-inch webbing for each thread.

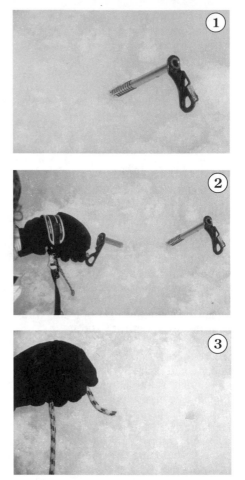

5. Better yet, grab the cord or webbing with a specialized Abalakov tool. The sharp hooked end on these tools makes grabbing the cord a cinch, and a rubber sheath protects your expensive shell gear from the hook when it's not in use.

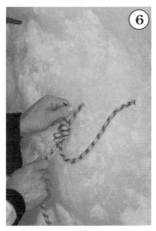

6. Tie the cord into a loop with a double Fisherman's knot.

7. Cut off the excess cord (if you haven't already prepared sections cut to length, which is a good idea).

8. Now thread your ropes through the cord . . .

9. . . . and rappel.

10. Of course, double Abalakov threads will be safer for rappeling. These cords could be slightly longer, to create a more shallow angle between them. For double Abalakovs, a length of 4 feet of cord might be better.

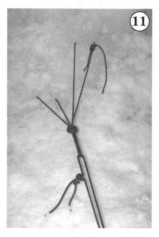

11. You can also thread double Abalakovs with a single piece of cord, and tie it off like a cordelette. This makes a bombproof rappel anchor.

For joining ropes together, an overhand knot is quick, and creates a low profile to help prevent the rope from snagging (though stuck ropes are more of a problem on rock than ice). Tie both strands together with an overhand knot as shown. Leaving an ample tail of at least 10 inches.

To ensure that the knot cannot creep, tie another overhand, this time in only one strand of rope, close to the double-strand overhand. Tighten both knots.

clipping loop of a wired nut. I've even managed to thread the cord with the pick of a tool, but this can be tricky and frustrating. Joe Josephson keeps a piece of stainless steel wire permanently attached to his pack for threading Abalakovs.

Cord threaded into the ice beats leaving ice screws, or aluminum pipe (an earlier tactic) for rappel anchors. Nonetheless, the cord or web is litter, so climbers should place V-threads no more than necessary. By late season, you can find dozens of V-threads "fixed" on some big routes in the Canadian Rockies.

Once you've established the anchors, it's time to rig the ropes for rappeling. If the rappel is less than half a rope length, use one rope for simplicity. Make sure you set the middle of the rope at the anchors, so one end won't be short. A middle mark on the rope is convenient for finding the rope's middle.

Usually you'll join two ropes so you have enough length for the rappel(s). At least four different knots exist for safely tying the ropes together. I often use a square knot backed up by two grapevines (the square grapevine), or an overhand knot. The overhand knot is gaining popularity for tying rappel lines because its low profile avoids rope snags, and it's quick to tie. To make the overhand knot fail-safe, keep the tails at least 6 inches

## Abalakov Sandwiches: The Facts

*by* Joe Josephson

Abalakov anchors have become hugely popular in Canada for descending and retreating from ice routes. They haven't caught on as much in the lower 48, because you can more often walk off or rappel from trees.

In 1990, Murray Toft and I tested Abalakov anchors. We found that properly built Abalakovs are bomber. In plastic ice, with 15 centimeters between the holes (the shortest distance I recommend), the average failure strength was 2,250 pounds. With a 20-centimeter span, average failure strength reached 2,900 pounds. These strengths are more than adequate for rappeling. Tested in cold, brittle conditions, the ice never failed; instead, the new 7-millimeter cord broke at an average of 3,250 pounds. These results indicate that the colder the ice, the stronger the anchor.

I regularly use 6-millimeter cord with no problem. For durability on popular climbs, use 7-millimeter cord, or better yet, old pieces of 8- or 9- millimeter rope. I precut my rappel cords with a hot knife, or use a lighter to melt the ends, to save the frustration of threading frayed cord through the holes.

For fast descents of multi-pitch routes lacking fixed rappel anchors: One person goes down first each time, carrying with them screws, wire, and cord. He or she sets one or two screws as backups, hangs from them, then builds the Abalakov. In wet ice the holes fill quickly with water. You can clear them by blowing through one of the holes. If the ice is brittle, you can often reduce plating by clearing the surface ice.

I often trust a single Abalakov, but two are definitely safer—never take any anchor system for granted. Practice building Abalakovs on the ground before relying on them for multi-pitch rappels. Only through experience, judgement, and constant observation can ice anchors be safe.

long. It's also wise to tie an extra overhand knot in one rope strand and snug it against the double-strand overhand, to prevent creeping. Another option for making this rappel knot more bomber is to tie two overhands right next to each other.

A standard belay/rappel plate or tube works well for rappeling ice routes, provided the ropes aren't too iced up. A figure-8 device works slightly better with iced ropes. If the ropes are completely iced, and you can't rig your rappel device, the standard Dulfersitz can work.

Rappeling also trashes expensive gloves, unless the palm is constructed of durable leather. If it's warm enough, I often take my brake hand glove off to spare it from the wear of the rappel. Some climbers carry a single leather glove for rappeling.

## Rappel Backups

So you're rappeling a multi-pitch icefall. The ropes knock an icicle loose which smashes your brake hand. With a rappel backup, you'll screech to a halt when you let go of the ropes; without a backup you'll accelerate into oblivion—your choice.

The autoblock is the quickest rappel backup to rig, especially when making multiple rappels, because the backup sling stays clipped to your leg loop. Six-millimeter perlon cord tied into a loop works well for rigging the autoblock, but I prefer a 9/16-inch shoulder-length sling, because it's a standard piece of gear with multiple uses. Spectra webbing works, but nylon creates better friction and has a higher melting temperature.

Keep the autoblock free of twists, and make sure you have a proper number of wraps around the ropes—four or five usually work well. Too many wraps give so much friction that you can barely move. Too few, and the autoblock won't engage when you need it. Keep the sling's stitching out of the autoblock, and retire your sling once it shows wear. When rappeling, hold the autoblock in your brake hand to keep it loose. The autoblock adds friction to your rappel, so you can more easily control your speed. If you let go, the autoblock locks onto the rope. This is handy when sorting out tangled rappel ropes. When locked, the autoblock never holds full body weight, just the weight held by your brake hand, so it's easy to loosen the autoblock to resume rappeling.

You can further increase your safety on rappel by knotting the ends of the ropes. Tying the rope ends together tangles the ropes—a separate large stopper knot in each rope works best. Having the rope ends knotted is especially important during bad weather, if it's dark, or if you're not very experienced. Be sure to untie the knots before pulling the ropes.

Once you're rigged and ready to rappel, don't forget to double check everything before you go. Check your harness buckle (and your partner's), the rappel device and locking carabiner, the anchor and the rope's attachment to it, and the knot joining the ropes. Finally, make a mental note of which rope to pull to retrieve the rappel lines.

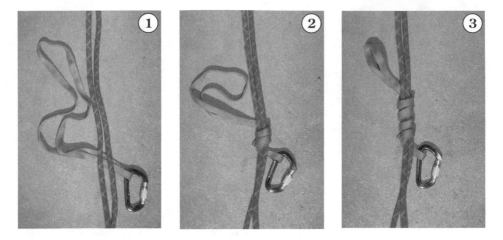

Backing up the rappel is always a good idea. To tie an autoblock, clip a shoulder-length sling or loop of cord to your leg loop, wrap it four or five times around the rappel ropes, . . .

. . . and clip it back to the carabiner.

As you rappel, keep the autoblock loose with your brake hand. It adds friction to your rappel, and if you begin to accelerate out-of-control, it halts you immediately.

During the rappel, the first person down should clear any hanging ice daggers before he or she passes below them, to avoid having these above the team. **Note: Don't knock off these daggers unless you're sure there are no parties below you.** If there are people below and you can't knock off the daggers, be extra gentle as you rappel over them—even the slightest touch could set them off. After rappeling, pull the ropes down immediately to prevent them from freezing into the ice.

An exciting rappel situation is the hanging rappel transfer, where no ledge exists and the climbing team hangs from the anchors while they rig the next rappel. It's nice to have a cow's tail—a sling or two girth-hitched to your harness—to hang from in this situation. The first climber down prepares the anchors, then inspects, clips, and tests them, and finally dismantles his or her rappel setup. The next climber then comes down, clips the anchors, and pulls the rope down, while the first climber feeds the rope for the next rappel. Be extra careful: double and triple check everything to make sure you've got it right, and don't drop the ropes!

## Lowering

When toproping, the climber often lowers back to the ground from the top of the pitch. Whenever you lean back to lower, first look down to make sure your belayer is with you; verbally communicate with him or her ("lower me"); and get your tools under control. A few climbers have suffered brutal falls because their belayers either took them off belay or weren't holding the rope when they leaned back to lower. I often hold onto the belayer's side of the rope as I begin to lower, until I'm convinced the belayer has me nice and tight.

The biggest *faux pas* when lowering someone is to drop them out of control, or to let the rope end pass through your belay device. Both of these potentially fatal mistakes have happened many times, even to experienced climbers. The lowering anchors must be within a half rope length for the climber to reach the ground, or you need two ropes. The belayer should also be tied into the rope, or at least have a knot tied in the end of the rope, so it can't go whistling through his or her belay device if the rope is too short. I use both hands for braking when lowering my partner.

## Retreating from a Pitch

Retreating from a pitch is simple if you have a bomber ice screw and are less than half a rope length out: simply leave a carabiner on the screw and lower to the ground or the belay. This method can get expensive if you retreat often, but it's quick and fail-safe, providing the top screw is solid. A less expensive alternative would be to build one, or better two, V-threads, and rappel or lower from these (obviously you would never lower with the rope running directly through the cord, because the rope will saw through the cord—you need to leave a carabiner or two and lower from them). If you're more than half a rope length up with only one rope, you'll have to build two sets of anchors and make two rappels to reach the belay.

A more nerve-wracking and dangerous retreat would involve downclimbing a pitch because you can't find good anchors. If you do this, you'll appreciate the times you practiced downclimbing.

## Retreating from a Route

Retreats arise from a variety of situations: bad weather, bad psyche, the team moving too slow, the climbing being too hard, or too dangerous—or worst of all, someone getting injured. Most retreats are routine: you just keep rappeling and leaving anchors until you get to the ground. If you climb long enough, especially on long routes, you're bound to suffer a few epic retreats.

When retreating you usually go down the route you came up, belay station to belay station, or natural anchor to natural anchor. Hopefully you're prepared with enough slings and cord to reach the ground. If not, you can always cut pieces out of your ropes to build Abalakov threads, provided you have your trusty knife. If not, hack the rope with an ice tool.

Dick Jackson on an early ascent of The Fang, Vail, Colorado.

# CHAPTER 9

# Hazards and Managing Risk

*by* Topher Donahue

To most people, hanging from great pillars of ice seems absurdly dangerous. The truth is, the biggest threats come from the surrounding environment, not from the wild features we climb.

Craig Luebben and I have spent many awesome days climbing together, yet we've backed off or changed plans nearly half the time due to uncontrollable hazards, or because things didn't feel right. Yet I consider the numerous retreats among my best successes, because I'm still alive, and I've gotten to climb some great routes without feeling like an accident waiting to happen. While you cannot eliminate risk, with patience and a #1 goal of returning home every time, a long life of great climbs can be yours for the taking.

In Phil Powers's book, *Wilderness Mountaineering*, he equates risk as being equal to exposure times probability. For example, passing quickly below other climbers causes much less exposure than climbing beneath them all day. When it's warm, the probability of a pillar collapsing is much greater than when it's cold. Waiting (years if necessary) until the probability of an accident is low, and minimizing exposure (changing plans if need be) are the keys to surviving.

## The Great White Monster

Sure, we could have more fun if it weren't for avalanches, but since they pose the single greatest hazard to ice climbers, we are forced to consider the beast. Every ice climb requires a substantial water source, which is often a large snowfield perched above the climb. When those snowfields release large slabs of snow instead of a little water, it's a fearsome display. One warm afternoon on the Icefields Parkway in Canada, we watched ten avalanches in 30 minutes pummel gullies that held climbs. Later we learned that three parties were swept off routes just days before. The best way to avoid such disaster is to learn the intricacies of avalanche forecasting and snow stability evaluation.

This text merely provides an overview of avalanche awareness. The responsible ice climber will take a class and read books to gain a basic knowledge of avalanches. We barely cover the beast here, because the subject is complex enough to merit a doctoral program. The *ABC of Avalanche Safety*, by E.R. LaChapelle, *Snow Sense* from the Alaska Mountain Safety Association, *Avalanche Safety for Skiers and Climbers* by Tony Daffern, and *Avalanche Aware* by John Moynier (Falcon Publishing) are recommended. Find out about a field course in your area from any ski patrol, the American Avalanche Institute 307-733-3315 in Wilson, Wyoming, or the Canadian Avalanche Centre 604-837-2435 in Revelstoke, British Columbia.

Whatever your level of training or experience, be wary of desire, and give yourself a wide margin for error at decision time. If no two snowflakes are alike, then no two avalanches are alike either.

## FACTORS CAUSING AVALANCHES

- **Trigger** Avalanches are usually triggered by weight or vibration. As little as a few more snowflakes, or as much as another avalanche, can cause a release. Frequently in avalanche accidents, the trigger is a human foot.
- **Slope Angle** Most large avalanches occur on slopes between 30 and 45 degrees, though in unstable conditions, slopes between 15 and 60 degrees can slide. Sloughs big enough to bury a human can happen on all but overhanging terrain. It's nice to know that some mountain features rarely avalanche, but slope angle is difficult to judge without an inclinometer, and unseen avalanches from above can threaten any slope.
- **Wind Loading** Wind blows snow onto leeward slopes and forms dangerous slabs even in gullies facing perpendicular to the wind. Wind loading can elevate the hazard from low to extreme in a few hours. Since a lot of ice forms in pronounced gullies, wind loading is often a concern.
- **New Snow** Large snowfalls always increase the danger. With time, however, the weight of the snow compresses the snowpack and stabilizes it. How long this takes depends on the type of snow, the underlying layers, and the air temperatures.
- **Temperature** Even slight temperature changes affect the snowpack, but radical changes, or unusually low or high temperatures, are more likely to bring everything tumbling down. Over time, warmer temperatures increase stability, and colder temperatures cause depth and surface hoar. Hoar, or temperature gradient snow, forms when the individual snowflakes crystallize to the consistency of sugar. This weak layer causes avalanches because it can't support the heavy snowpack that comes later in the season. Dig into any early season snowpack, and you'll probably find depth hoar near the ground where the cold winter air meets the warmer earth. Surface hoar forms at the top of the snowpack, and creates a weak layer after it is buried by new snow.
- **Layering** Snow falling over the course of the winter sets up in layers. Slab avalanches result when these different layers within the snowpack don't bond well. Imagine a 5-acre wide, 6-foot thick sandwich with extra mayonnaise on a plate tilted at 35 degrees—not a very balanced lunch.
- **Terrain** Ice climbers often find themselves in terrain traps, such as steep, narrow valleys where even a small avalanche can be fatal. The approach to the *Rigid Designator* in Vail is a perfect example: the slopes above lie between 30 and 45 degrees, and a slide will be funneled onto approaching climbers. *Whiteman Falls* in Alberta is considered low hazard, yet the approach

follows a narrow ravine where a small slough could spell The End, especially if your partner is far ahead or without a shovel. Ridges are often safer, but occasionally the tension in a slab avalanche will even release snow from a ridgeline.

• **Sunshine** Direct sun on a snowpack can weaken the bonding and change a low-level hazard into a high hazard very quickly.

• **Rain** During late season, rain on the snowpack both increases the load and can undermine the bonding within the snowpack. If it's raining, stay away from even mildly dangerous snow slopes.

• **Glaciers** Glaciers have their own avalanche personality, and "rolling the dice" is how climbers speak of passing under, or climbing on, unstable glacial formations, such as seracs.

## Sleuthing to Survive

Do your homework! Learn how to evaluate the stability of the snowpack. Some mountain regions have excellent avalanche forecasting systems; the Canadian Rockies have one of the best systems in North America, and it's available over the phone. (The number is listed in the Appendix.) Check the avalanche forecast! Believe it! Continuously evaluate conditions instead of making a single decision and going with it. Some things to watch for include recent heavy snowfalls, sudden warming trends, recent wind loading, 'whumphing' sounds and settlements on any angle terrain, a hollow-feeling snowpack, cracks shooting through the snow, and, most importantly, signs of recent slides on similar slopes. On big alpine climbs, watching the objective for at least 24 hours, to see what comes down where, is standard practice.

When moving through exposed avalanche terrain, remove pole or ice axe leashes from wrists, unfasten ski safety straps, travel one at a time through the danger zone, and watch each other. Experts used to suggest unbuckling your pack's waist belt and ditching your pack in a slide to facilitate swimming. Now they suggest leaving your pack on as protection against rocks and trees. You make the call. Short sections of exposed terrain can be navigated more safely by pulling out the rope and staying anchored to rocks or trees.

If you're caught in an avalanche, try to hang onto something secure while the slide rips past. The force of gravity-driven snow will overwhelm the strongest climber, though, so if you can't hang onto something, swim like a gold medalist to stay on top of the snow. When the snow starts slowing, get your hands in front of your face to make an air cavity, because if you are buried when the avalanche stops, you won't be able to move.

In avalanche country, always carry probe poles, shovel, and an avalanche rescue beacon, and know how to use them.

## Don't Climb Anything You Wouldn't Stand Under

Ice is amazingly strong and tenacious. Today's best climbers hang from icicles barely bigger than their bodies, and a fist-sized patch of ice stuck in a corner will hold the fattest climber if used correctly. But even Alex Lowe, who reads ice as well as anyone, misjudged the strength of an icicle, and rode it 70 feet to the ground. Tales of massive pillars falling after someone rigged a timely retreat speak for always heeding your best judgement.

Some formations are less stable than others. These include free hanging pillars, icicles, seracs, any steep snow features, and cornices. Formations that are poorly bonded to the rock are some of the most dangerous. Before climbing, closely observe the edges of the route for water running between the ice and rock. If there is, or if temperatures have been unusually warm, don't climb delicate formations. Direct sunshine can warm and destabilize the ice, increase the amount of running water, and even melt out your screw placements, particularly late in the season or in warmer climates. Icicles may fall and even whole climbs can collapse.

Bruce Hendricks, a master of Canadian Rockies horror shows, has a unique method of testing seemingly fragile structures. He whacks the structure as hard as possible with the side of his tool. If it moves, he goes home. If it makes noise, he thinks twice; if he decides to climb, he treads very lightly. If it does neither, he considers it solid (a relative term, no doubt), and never looks back. This is a valuable technique for smaller structures, but giant hanging icicles may seem sturdy until you hit them at their attachment to the rock, and the whole thing releases.

Climbers are one of the least stable features in the ice environment—they can fall at any time! Belay out of the potential trajectory of their crampons and tools, because perforated belayers don't hold ropes.

### "Ice!!"

Once I was hit hard enough by falling ice to break buckles on my backpack. If at all possible, put the belay in a protected place, or move to one before the next lead. At some point, however, we all have to belay in the firing line; when it happens, stay upright, because if you duck it exposes your back and neck to the barrage. Hide beneath your pack if possible. Even if the belayer is protected when

*Secret Probation, Vail, Colorado.*

you're dropping the bomb, always yell "ICE!" to alert everyone below.

If your belayer or another party is not looking up your barrel, knock off dinner plates caused by botched placements. This keeps you from standing on them, and clears the unstable ice for other climbers. When rappeling, knock off icicles and thin curtains before going below them, lest the rope send them towards your skull after you pass by. Generally, though, destroy as little ice as possible.

Most falling ice is caused by other climbers. As tempting as it can be, never climb below others. Inevitably, angstful people will climb below you. Being patient, courteous, and creative with route finding are perhaps the greatest challenges to some ice climbers. While guiding, I find animosity and inconsiderate behavior all too common in beginner areas. But on the big nasties, where only the best climbers venture, the creative route finding, teamwork, consideration, and patience among rope teams is usually brilliant. When climbing in popular areas, get up earlier than everyone else and expect to work with others to give everyone a chance to climb in a safe, positive atmosphere.

Negative energy and actions only give land owners and legislators more reasons to limit access to our environmentally friendly sport, and makes it harder for ice parks to be developed to ease the pressures of too many climbers on too little ice.

## Extreme Cold

**Staying warm = insulation + metabolism + hydration + fuel + activity.** Consider all parts of the equation when heading out on cold days, and take the time to solve problems before they escalate. Drink (not alcohol) and eat well the night before the climb. Move around on belays before you get cold, bring heat packs for hands, take spare mittens, loosen boot laces to the sloppy point, and know the limits of your gear. A down parka can make the difference between misery and fun. When climbing, expect brittle ice, broken picks, and metal objects to freeze to wet skin instantly (don't use your mouth to hold a carabiner when placing pro), and a fast deterioration from fun to epic if small mistakes are made. Practice for such conditions by wearing heavy gloves or mittens on warmer days to learn different systems for placing pro, and understand your limits with less dexterity. Most importantly, monitor each other for frostbite, hypothermia, and general well-being.

## Darkness

Headlamps are standard gear on any multi-pitch route, or routes requiring a long approach. It's even a good idea to have one along on a day of roadside cragging. You never know when your rope's going to get stuck, or some other problem will delay you, and on short winter days, darkness comes on fast. You can rarely start a climb or approach too early, but so often we seem to start too late.

### Forced Bivies

In the winter, living through an unplanned bivouac takes a mighty effort. Use body heat, huddle together, take a space blanket (some climbers stuff one of these in the suspension of their helmet), or even better, a bivi sack. Keep moving to stay warm—Peter Croft once rolled boulders all night to stay warm during a forced bivouac. If you're not on technical terrain, remove your crampons so they don't conduct heat away from your feet. A down jacket and a snowcave give you a chance of making it through most anything, but you don't want to test the theory.

### Storms

The intensity and longevity of winter storms bring harsh treatment to anyone caught in an exposed place. Eighty percent of avalanches occur during storms or in the following 24 hours, and a similar percent of mountaineering disasters happen in the same time frame. Whiteouts, frozen ropes or fingers, deep snow, or exhaustion can make escaping a bad situation nearly impossible. Study the mountain for paths of escape, and for landmarks to navigate by if visibility decreases. Bring a map and compass, or even a GPS, and know how to use them.

A little research about the type and probability of storm in a given area is invaluable, as it helps you make decisions and be prepared. Check the weather forecast before a winter climb, but remember that a general forecast may be off the mark from the true mountain weather.

### Leader Falls

In some ways, ice climbing is more akin to kayaking than to rock climbing when it comes to making mistakes and pushing your limits. It's best to lead dozens of pitches at each level before upping your standard, just as a wise kayaker slowly challenges wilder and less forgiving rapids. In rock climbing, falling is often safe and may even help you relax, but ice is totally different. Other than on new-age mixed climbs, most ice climbers avoid falling on lead *at all costs*. A leader fall without injury should be counted as quite lucky. If you fall, do everything in your power to keep your crampons away from the ice and your tools in your grasp.

### Descents

The best thing about descending ice climbs is that wherever thick, solid ice exists, a rappel anchor can be arranged. The worst thing is that nothing can be counted on. Anchors can be buried in the ice one year, and out of reach the next. Walk-offs can be avalanche prone, and whiteouts, exhaustion, and short winter days make descending from big climbs a serious proposition. If you venture outside cragging areas, know how to use Abalakovs (see Chapter 8), be prepared to set your own anchors, research the descent, carry a headlamp, and save some battery juice for the way down.

## Fixed Rock Anchors

Be suspicious of all fixed anchors. The presence of a fixed anchor doesn't mean it is solid or that the person who put it in knew what he or she was doing. On top of that, the rock in popular ice areas is often dubious. Repeated freeze/thaw cycles of winter loosen fixed pitons, and constant wetness corrodes pins, bolts and hangers. Check pitons to ensure that they are still solid, and be sure that the rock around them is not loose. Do not pound on bolts—this weakens them; rather, visually inspect the placement and the hanger, and make sure the bolt is tight in its hole.

One pull of a rope through a rappel sling can significantly weaken the sling. So does exposure to UV radiation from the sun, and sometimes rodents chew on rappel slings. Replace rappel slings if they are at all faded or frayed, and make sure your new rigging equalizes the load on the rappel anchors. Cut off the old slings and take them with you.

If you're rappeling from a tree, make sure it is alive, well rooted, and large enough to easily support your weight. Beware of single anchor points, poorly tied or improper knots, and the frightfully common "American triangle", where the webbing is rigged through all the anchors in a large triangle. Rather than equalizing the load on the anchors, the American triangle increases the load.

## Glaciers

Glaciated regions offer some of the most magnificent ice climbs on earth, so the skills required to safely navigate glaciers are worth knowing. Glacier travel is its own discipline of climbing. Rather than present a brief treatment of this extensive material, we refer the reader to Andy Selters's *Glacier Travel and Crevasse Rescue*, and we recommend taking a glacier travel course from a respected guide service. Because of the unforgiving hazards on glaciers—namely crevasses, bergschrunds, and icefalls—it's very unwise to travel on glaciers without this specialized knowledge.

## Inconsistent Ratings

Ice ratings are inherently inaccurate, and taking them literally can be dangerous. Don't climb something that looks desperate just because it's graded within your limit—a WI4 pitch can be WI6 if conditions are bad.

### Sixth Sense

Most climbers develop a sixth sense, which gives them a subtle warning of approaching danger. Never ignore this inner voice— if things don't *feel* right, get out of there. Whether the reason is avalanches, crowds, an approaching storm, or unusual conditions, decide not to climb! Turning around is a bigger success than climbing when you suspect it's not safe. Like Bob Marley sings, "The man who runs away, lives to fight another day."

### Self-Rescue

As mentioned at the beginning of this book, it's absolutely essential that you learn self-rescue techniques before venturing into the big wild, in case things go wrong. These involved techniques must be learned and practiced before you need them. Never count on rescuers being able to save you—conditions may be too harsh for them to reach you, or you may be all alone, with no way to call for a rescue. Seek outside rescue only as a last resort. On this note, while many self-reliant climbers hate cellular phones and radios, these devices have saved lives—and they've also been abused, calling for unnecessary rescues.

# North American Ice: A Brief Overview

*by* Topher Donahue

This chapter closes the book with a brief look at what this continent has to offer. Waterfall climbing has grown up in North America, and the multitude of proving grounds have produced many talented ice climbers. This is not a guidebook, or even a list of all the areas, but rather a Big Daddy hit list with a note on what to expect when you get there. Research every area thoroughly before moving a tool.

Bill Belcourt on
The White Angel,
Santaquin Canyon.

JOHN BARSTOW PHOTO

## CANADIAN ROCKIES

This vast area, shared by British Columbia and Alberta, sets the standard by which all the world's ice playgrounds are measured. The avalanche hazard on many Rockies climbs can be extreme, so patience and religious use of avalanche forecasts are essential. Loaded with everything from massive moderates to nightmarish slender pillars, from hard mixed routes to 1,000-meter marathons, the Rockies will change any climber's perspective of ice climbing.

## CODY, WYOMING

Cody has less snowfall than most ice climbing areas, porous stone, plentiful ground water, cheap lodging, minimal avalanche hazard, a long and consistent season, and the ice is often fat and blue. All levels of difficulty can be found on aesthetic multi-pitch flows. Need we say more?

## HYALITE CANYON, MONTANA

In early season you can drive to the this area, but later the road becomes impassable. Then you have an option: 10 miles (each way) on a snowmobile, or a brutal day on skis. Most of the ice comes from seeps on the canyon walls that form fat pillars in wild places. Hyalite has one of the best collections of hard mixed routes, thanks to Alex Lowe. The avalanche danger can be extreme on the many climbs that form in gullies.

## NEW HAMPSHIRE

Mount Washington provides alpine flavor on the East Coast, with potentially high avalanche hazard, vicious storms, and 1,000-foot climbs. The steep ice of Frankenstein Cliff compliments the mixed routes of Cannon Cliff and Cathedral Ledges to make the northeast an excellent place to play the icy game. Even better, most places, except Cannon and Mount Washington, have minimal avalanche hazard.

## ORIENT BAY, ONTARIO

Many single-pitch climbs at every level can be found here, and there is no avalanche hazard. A long season makes for predictable conditions, but be ready to wade through bottomless depth hoar to reach the climbs.

## QUEBEC

Although this region is known for mind-boggling climbs like the long *Pomme D'Or*, Quebec ice is more often sampled at the Pont Rouge area where single pitch routes on wild pillars of all grades can be found. The north shore of the Saint Lawrence has some big ice, and the Gaspé Peninsula has over 50 roadside classics, up to three pitches long. Avalanche hazard on many routes is minimal.

## ROCKY MOUNTAIN NATIONAL PARK, COLORADO

This alpine ice, and obligatory avalanche considerations, can be found every month of the year. Spring and fall conditions form excellent mixed climbing, but winter can be windy with brittle ice, especially on the routes above treeline. The easier climbs are extremely popular, while the hard ones are frequented by a patient few who know where to look.

## SAN JUANS, COLORADO

The heart of Colorado ice. Ouray's famous ice park, the megaclassics near Telluride, and numerous long climbs around Silverton are but a few of the options. The flows are well fed, both naturally and artificially, so they recover well from abuse, and the local communities understand the pursuit of mountain adventure better than most. Avalanche hazard in many areas is extreme.

## SIERRA, CALIFORNIA

(contributed by John Moynier)

The abundant snowfall and high elevations of the High Sierra combine to produce a decent variety of both waterfall and alpine ice. The most popular areas are found in the Palisades region, as well as Lee Vining Canyon near Yosemite Park. These areas are also significant from a historical perspective as they were a testing ground for Yvon Chouinard and Doug Robinson's equipment and technique breakthroughs in the late 1960s. Yosemite Valley is home to many spectacular waterfalls that form up on occasion, including the *Widow's Tears*. The Lake Tahoe region also has a number of fine areas, including Lover's Leap, Coldstream Canyon and the Kirkwood area. Finally, Tahquitz Rock in southern California occasionally produces some long, hard routes.

## VAIL, COLORADO

Perhaps the most overpublicized ice in the world. Vail does have some great routes, though, from fat-ice classics to dicey mixed routes to athletic sport-ice routes which involve desperate rock-hooking and trivial ice climbing. Most climbs are one pitch long and form every year. All the areas have some degree of avalanche danger on the approach.

## VALDEZ, ALASKA

Plentiful water, perfect terrain, and easy approaches make Valdez a great ice climbing destination. Many of the best routes are right off the highway outside town, and locals are friendly about giving advice. Valdez is not overrun with climbers like many areas in the lower 48. The area also holds some of the best backcountry skiing imaginable. Expect moderate to high avalanche danger.

## VERMONT

A multitude of classic three-pitch ice faces and vertical pillars grace Lake Willoughby. According to Joe Josephson, this may be the single greatest ice climbing cliff on Earth. What more can one say?

## WASATCH RANGE AND VICINITY, UTAH

The sticky Utah ice is plentiful and fun to climb, but often it comes and goes several times each season. Between Big Cottonwood Canyon in the north and Maple Canyon in the south, enough ice forms to keep a large posse of Salt Lake City climbers busy with new routes every winter. Maple Canyon and vicinity may prove to be one of the best mixed and thin-ice venues in North America. Be sure to avoid the sudden warm spells that plague the area, and beware the high avalanche danger presented by the huge snowfalls. I've lost two good friends to the great white monster in the Wasatch.

# Appendix

## REFERENCES

*The ABC of Avalanche Safety,* E.R. LaChapelle. A short study of the great white monster.

*Accidents in North American Mountaineering.* Published every year. Required reading for learning from others' mistakes and misfortunes.

*Advanced Rock Climbing,* John Long and Craig Luebben (Falcon Publishing). Crucial information on advanced ropework, climbing techniques, and a detailed presentation of self rescue techniques.

*Allen and Mike's Really Cool Backcountry Ski Book,* Allen O'Bannon and Mike Clelland. A complete guide to traveling and camping skills for a winter environment.

*Avalanche Aware,* John Moynier (Falcon Publishing). Covers safe travel techniques in avalanche terrain. A revision of the Chockstone Press book *Avalanche Awareness.*

*Avalanche Safety for Skiers and Climbers,* Tony Daffern.

*Better Bouldering* and *Stone Crusade,* John Sherman, for when you're tired of harsh temperatures.

*Climbing Anchors* and *More Climbing Anchors,* John Long (Falcon Publishing). Excellent, detailed presentations of rock climbing anchor systems and riggings.

*Climbing Ice,* Yvon Chouinard. The all-time classic.

*Glacier Travel and Crevasse Rescue,* Andy Selters. Essential information for those traveling in glacial terrain.

*How to Rock Climb,* John Long (Falcon Publishing). The single best resource on basic rock climbing techniques and ropework.

*Ice World,* Jeff Lowe. Chronicles Jeff Lowes ice climbing career, and gives many tips on alpine and waterfall ice climbing.

*Knots for Climbers,* Craig Luebben (Falcon Publishing). Shows all of the climbing knots you'll ever need, and a few that you won't.

*Mountaineering, Freedom of the Hills,* Graydon and Hanson, editors. The best single reference for all-around mountaineering and alpine climbing knowledge.

*Self Rescue,* David Fasulo. Detailed information on rescuing your team from many bad situations.

*Snow Sense,* Alaska Mountain Safety Association.

## RESOURCES

American Mountain Guides Association
710 Tenth St.
Golden, CO 80401
(303) 271-0984
E-mail: news@amga.com
Web site: www.amga.com

Association of Canadian Mountain Guides (ACMG)
P.O. Box 8341
Canmore, AB, T1W 2V1
CANADA
(403) 678-2885
E-mail: acmg@telusplanet.net
Web site: www.acmg.ca

American Avalanche Institute
P.O. Box 308
Wilson, Wyoming 83014
(307) 733-3315
E-mail: aai@wyoming.com

Canadian Avalanche Centre
P.O. Box 2759
Revelstoke, BC, V0E250
CANADA
(250) 837-2435

Canadian Rockies Avalanche Forecast
(800) 667-1105 from Canada
(604) 290-9333 from US

## GLOSSARY

**aid:** pulling or hanging on equipment rather than climbing with the action of hands, feet, and body English to get up a climb.
**anchor:** a mechanical attachment that secures climbers to a cliff.
**arete:** an outside corner of rock.
**armbar, armlock:** a means of holding onto a wide crack.
**belay:** securing a climber with a rope.
**beta:** detailed route information, sometimes move by move.
**bergschrund:** gap where a glacier meets rock.
**biners:** see carabiners.
**bollard:** a naturally constructed ice and snow anchor.
**bolt:** an artificial anchor placed in a hole drilled for that purpose.
**bomber or bomb-proof:** absolutely fail-safe.
**cam:** to lodge in a crack by counterpressure: that which lodges.
**carabiners:** aluminum alloy rings equipped with a spring-loaded snap gate; called biners.
**ceiling:** an overhang of sufficient size to loom overhead.
**chock:** a wedge or mechanical device that provides an anchor in a rock crack.
**chockstone:** a rock lodged in a crack.

**clean:** a description of routes that may be variously free of vegetation, loose rock, or the need to place pitons; also the act of removing chocks from a pitch.

**crampon:** metal spikes that attach to climbing boots and provide traction on ice and snow.

**crimper:** a small but positive edge.

**crux:** the most difficult section of a climb or pitch.

**dihedral:** an inside corner of rock.

**drag:** usually used in reference to the resistance of rope through carabiners.

**Dulfersitz:** a method of rappelling that involves wrapping the rope around the body and using the resulting friction.

**dynamic or dyno:** a lunge move.

**edge:** a small rock ledge, or the act of standing on an edge.

**exposure:** that relative situation where a climb has particularly noticeable sheerness.

**fifi:** an un-gated hook used to quickly attach a climber to an anchor.

**figure-eight:** a knot used in climbing free.

**free climb or free ascent:** to climb using hands and feet only; the rope is only used to safeguard against injury, not for upward progress or resting.

**French technique:** a method of ascending and descending low angle ice and snow with crampons.

**glissade:** to slide down a snowfield on one's rump or feet.

**gobis:** hand abrasions.

**hangdog:** when a leader hangs from a piece of protection to rest, then continues on without lowering back to the ground; not a free ascent.

**jam:** wedging feet, hands, fingers or other body parts to gain purchase in a crack.

**jugs:** big hand holds.

**lead:** to be first on a climb, placing protection to safeguard a fall.

**lieback:** the climbing maneuver that entails pulling with the hands while pushing with the feet.

**line:** the path of weakness in the rock; usually the route.

**mantle:** the climbing maneuver used to gain a single feature above one's head.

**monodoigts:** very small holes or holds, about finger size.

**move:** movement; one of a series of motions necessary to gain climbing distance.

**on-sight:** to climb a route without prior knowledge or experience of the moves, and without falling or otherwise weighting the rope (also on-sight flash).

**opposition:** nuts, anchors, or climbing maneuvers that are held in place by the simultaneous stress of two forces working against each other.

**pinkpoint:** to lead (without falling) a climb that has been pre-protected with anchors rigged with carabiners.

**pins:** pitons.

**pitch:** the section of rock between belays.

**pitons:** metal spikes of various shapes, hammered into the rock to provide anchors in cracks (also pins or pegs).

**placement:** the quality of a nut or anchor.

**protection or pro:** the anchors used to safeguard the leader.

**prusik:** both the knot (n.) and any means by which one mechanically ascends a rope (v.).

**quickdraws:** short slings with biners that help provide drag-free rope management for the leader.

**rappel:** to descend a rope by means of mechanical brake devices.

**redpoint:** to lead a route, clipping protection as you go, without falling or resting on pro.

**RP:** small nut used mostly in aid climbing.

**runout:** the distance between two points of protection; often referring to a long stretch of climbing without protection.

**Screamers (Yates Screamers):** load-limiting quickdraws that are sewn in such a manner as to lessen the force of a fall.

**second:** the second person on a rope team, usually also the leaders belayer.

**self-arrest:** a method of stopping a fall on steep snow or low angle ice.

**sling or runner:** a webbing loop used for a variety of purposes to anchor to the rock.

**smear:** to stand on the front of the foot and gain friction against the rock across the breadth of the sole, the point being to adhere to the rock.

**stance:** a standing rest spot, often the sight of the belay.

**stem:** to bridge between two widely-spaced holds.

**Supergaiters:** gaiters that enclose the entire boot.

**thin:** a climb or hold of relatively featureless character.

**toprope:** a belay from an anchor point above; protects the climber from falling even a short distance.

**traverse:** to move sideways, without altitude gain.

**verglas:** extremely thin ice plastered to rock.

**wall or big wall:** a long climb traditionally done over multiple days, but may take just a few hours for ace climbers.